TV FAQ

John Ellis

I.B. TAURIS

LONDON · NEW YORK

Published in 2007 by I.B.Tauris & Co Ltd
6 Salem Road, London W2 4BU
175 Fifth Avenue, New York NY 10010
www.ibtauris.com

In the United States of America and in Canada distributed by
Palgrave Macmillan, a division of St Martin's Press
175 Fifth Avenue, New York NY 10010

ISBN 978 1 84511 565 4

A full CIP record for this book is available from the British Library
A full CIP record for this book is available from the Library of
Congress

Library of Congress catalog card: available

Typeset in Basset by Steve Tribe, Andover
Printed and bound in India by Thomson Press India Limited

Contents

Questions about TV as a medium

What is this book about?

This book tries to answer common questions about TV as we find it in the first decade of the twenty-first century. These stretch from the political, ethical and cultural to the technological and industrial and the plain inconsequential. Yet they all illuminate an aspect of the complicated modern phenomenon that is television. They all relate to each other, directly or indirectly, as is shown by the frequent cross-references between sections indicated by a '**»**'. Television as a social phenomenon is difficult to comprehend because it involves technology, politics and entertainment, yet TV itself is such an everyday, taken-for-granted medium. A lot of what it does is supremely unimportant yet, at the same time, TV is the primary source of much of our information about and impressions of the wider world. If **» Q5, Q6** modern society has become a mediatised society,**»** then television has been central in that transformation. The vast majority of people watch TV almost every day and for **» Q8, Q11** substantial amounts of time.**»** It brings vital information, the problems and disasters of the day, along with much that seems trivial or mundane. Many of the problems of understanding TV come from regarding these as conflicting activities, rather than tracing the interrelations between the two. Politics has been transformed by the growth in psychological understanding that has developed **» Q7** in TV dramas, soaps and chat shows.**»**

Television can be found everywhere in modern society; it provides much of our entertainment and information about the wider world; yet it is still regarded as an inferior medium. There is plenty of bad TV about – some of it astonishingly inept – just as there are plenty of bad paintings. Hardly anyone rejects painting as a medium on the basis of those bad examples, yet some feel able to reject TV as a medium based on the dissatisfaction or revulsion aroused in them by some of its programming. Much writing about TV, both popular and academic, treats the medium in disparaging tones. Many of these criticisms tend to assume that TV could do things for which, as a medium, it is ill-suited: to explain or even solve the important issues of the day, to be consistently inoffensive or even to uphold particular public moral standards. That TV is expected to do these things is partially the fault of the medium itself in its past and current forms. TV is a medium that aspires to cover everything and to be accessible to everyone. It aims to be universal in its reach, inclusive in its coverage and intelligible to everyone. Not surprisingly, it fails to present complex arguments well.**»**

It is also a medium that regularly fails to take a moral stance. Individual programmes can be fiercely moralistic in tone, or can flout moral conventions.**»** As an entertainment medium, TV sometimes seeks to shock. As a medium of information, it generally tries to avoid didacticism and preaching. As a result, TV tends to be morally ambivalent. Many TV programmes, both fictional and factual, show things and suspend explicit judgement on them, within the bounds of a wide consensus about what constitutes socially acceptable behaviour. Within these boundaries, evil characters tend to be understandable, and good characters are hard to find. Beyond the boundaries, however, lies an undifferentiated evil populated by al-Qaeda, teenage hoodlums and paedophiles alike. TV as a medium suspends moral judgement within the boundaries, but seldom explores beyond them. And these boundaries differ depending on the national culture that is involved. TV is not so much *im*moral as *a*moral. It shows a wide range of social attitudes, and can tend towards the sensationalist. But the come-ons often seem worse than the actual programmes. The idea of the Big Brother house with its round-the-clock surveillance was greeted with horror before people saw it; when they got the idea, they criticised it for its great stretches of tedium and trivia. Indeed, compared to cinema, novels or newspapers, TV contains a remarkable amount of mundane material.

Television is also a medium of the moment. It is convenient to use, always available at the touch of a button. The majority of its programming addresses the moment in which we live.**»** This is at once the strength and weakness of television. It makes it a medium that addresses people

Q1 What is this book about?

as it finds them, in their everyday lives. It relates to the common comings and goings of life, designing its programming to fit the concerns of the moment and the patterns of daily, weekly and seasonal change.**》** Yet it also makes television seem like an ephemeral medium, of no lasting value.**》** I prefer to see television as a medium that is temporarily meaningful. Many programmes contain allusions to the moment in which they co-exist with their audiences, to the extent that the passing of time makes them hard to understand: many programmes from the 1950s are more incomprehensible now than are novels from the nineteenth century.**》** Yet the temporarily meaningful nature of television is also its strength as a medium. Several of the questions in this book relate to the feelings of connection with television that are produced by this address to the present moment. It lies behind the particular ways that TV entertainment and drama have developed, producing genres like the sitcom, the long drama series and the soap opera.

》 Q38

》 Q32

》 Q35

The temporary nature of most television output may blind us to its role in transforming modern society. Television has been part of wider trends towards developing a consumerist society (by promoting its trappings through adverts and programmes) and a more personalised society (by developing discourses and understandings of the emotions). Television has also mediated the increasing complexity of modern life to modern citizens. It has shown their myriad of problems with technology and personal behaviour, the intergenerational conflicts, the cheats and rip-off merchants, the frustrated and violent, those who understand too little and those who know the truth only too well. Television has not been the cause of this increasing complexity of life. As a pervasive and everyday medium, it has been central in mediating it to the widest possible number of people.

Now, it seems possible that television will lose that centrality. The Internet is providing new means of providing moving images and sounds when and where they are demanded. In some areas, television is adapting; in others it is being swept away. Television has always been a one-way medium, providing material for an audience with no substantial means of returning the favour or disputing what they get. Television broadcasters are finding some of this interactivity by extending their operations to include the Internet. Yet the Internet in its current form and patterns of use does not easily encompass some of the major characteristics of television. It does not easily support sustained narratives, for instance. Instead it delivers television narratives (or summaries of them) through download and streaming sites.**»** It is also a medium that requires a more active and engaged process of search and selection, a clear understanding of what you want before you can get it. TV provides 'always-on' flows of material that might be of interest now. TV will be finished only when the population as a whole turns instinctively to another medium just to see what's on.

» Q46

Television is an extensive and pervasive medium. Any one person can watch only a tiny proportion of the output that is nowadays available to them, but everyone has views and questions about the medium as a whole. This book examines the whole phenomenon of television as it is found in UK and similar countries today. It tries to answer many of the questions about television that I have been asked frequently over the years, and the main assertions about the medium that are generally held to be true. Often the most basic questions have proved to be the most illuminating. The questions are grouped together so that the book could be read sequentially as an attempt to outline the main features of the medium. The questions are organised into four sections, but many of the answers refer the reader on to other questions and answers that are often in different sections of the book. The first section confronts some of the major generalisations about television, how it behaves as a medium and how it affects both individuals and society. The second section looks at the major genres of television and how they operate. This and the following sections contain many details that develop the arguments put forward in general terms in the first section. The third section contains questions that relate to the everyday use of television, and the fourth

Q1 What is this book about?

questions relating to how the TV industry works and the technologies that we use to access its products.

In a book such as this, which ranges widely, it is impossible to acknowledge, even in a bibliography, all the works that have been important to me in the burgeoning areas of television studies, media studies and cultural and communications studies. Nor is it possible to acknowledge all the TV professionals whose information has been invaluable. Many therefore must remain unthanked. However, some discussions have been particularly important during the rather long period it has taken to devise and write this book. These include Royal Holloway, University of London; the Southern Broadcast History Group; the two symposia on the 'End of TV' organised by Elihu Katz and Paddy Scannell; and joint AHRC/BBC events organised by Rob Turnock. The questions themselves have developed from those asked by students at Royal Holloway, or solicited by me from friends and family. Some of the most ingenious ones have been a revelation to me, as I had not previously seen TV from the point of view that they implied. I am particularly grateful to my most perceptive critics: my son and daughter Carl and Harriet and, above all, my partner Rosalind Coward. This book is dedicated to them with my heartfelt thanks for all their care and attention.

Q2 What is 'television'?

In 1980, this would have seemed a pointless question. Even in 1990, the answer was pretty obvious. Television was what you got from your TV set at home: a number of channels that scheduled programmes, events and films at particular times, some for free and some for a subscription. Now the question is becoming more difficult to answer, as all the background assumptions still made in 1990 are being challenged. TV comes over the Internet, over mobile phones, over screens in public spaces. TV can come when you want it, on demand rather than as a scheduled stream. TV no longer necessarily consists of 'programmes' since the development of all kinds of extra material, from text alerts to mobiles, interactive buttons leading to further material, exclusive material for mobiles, websites, subscribers and so on. TV is not just what is provided by broadcasters, as these new forms allow non-broadcasters to provide access to material. Production companies deal directly with viewers through websites. Advertisers use screens in public spaces. Cameras stare down at us in public spaces, relaying images (usually soundless) to screens and recording devices somewhere or other, for someone or other to watch. Phone companies provide audio-visual material for their 3G subscribers, including material like adverts, travel or even historical information that relates specifically to the place where the user is located. Non-professionals who have made something interesting email their material or put it onto websites like YouTube for anyone who cares to watch, which many do. An explosion of audio-visual material is beginning, evidenced by the use of camera-phones to document news events and by the increasing sophistication of so-called 'amateur' productions. Gone are the days when 'the tube' or 'the box' could be nicknames for the TV, as tubes and boxes have proliferated beyond anything that could remotely be called TV, and new means of creating, accessing and looking at material are creating new-screen viewers who are different from TV viewers.

TV always was just one application of a technology. The

inventors of that technology saw all kinds of applications for this device that would enable 'far-seeing'. They saw the potential for video-phones, for education at a distance, for surveillance, for live cinema. It was perhaps John Logie Baird's particular genius to realise that the technology had a key potential: to bring entertainment and information into ordinary homes, just as radio was doing in the 1920s. So the technology was harnessed for broadcasting, so much so that other uses were neglected, and television became synonymous with broadcasting.

There is much to be said for retaining this link, for saying that television means the broadcasting from a central place to many screens of scheduled material that is current or contemporary and is of general interest. Television as traditionally conceived has four main characteristics. It is *broadcast*, using a 'push' medium in which the choice for the viewer is less what to watch than which service or channel to watch. So it is distinct from any 'pull' medium, in which the user actively chooses what they want to watch at a particular moment from a library of constantly available material. It is *universal* in the sense that it is addressed to everyone in general. This does not mean that it expects everyone to be interested, but rather that everything is deliberately made to be comprehensible to the general population, should they be interested. This distinguishes it from more targeted media, including websites and magazines, which can often use a specialised vocabulary or set of references, and provide no particular means of understanding them. With this goes the *normality* of the familiar regular schedule in which those programmes are fitted, and in which they gain their universal acceptance as a common reference point between people. Finally, television as traditionally conceived is a *time-tied* medium, in which material has a certain period of currency which declines quite rapidly. For a news broadcast this can be a matter of hours or even minutes as stories develop. A sporting event or a football match is current for just as long as it is live. As soon as the result is known, people refer to it in the past tense; it is history. For an episode of a soap or a chat show, the period of currency can be two or three days, until the next episode or until the momentary frisson of revelation has lost its edge. An episode of a primetime drama series will be current until the next episode is released, normally a week later. The latest episode of anything on TV has a considerable premium.

There are problems with limiting the definition of television just to this traditional model. The programmes themselves constantly escape from the confines of this kind of TV, even if they were made for it. For years, they have been sold on VHS and DVD after their main broadcast life was over. Old television programmes can now be accessed through the web on demand; new television programmes relate closely to other kinds of TV material through red button links. Broadcasters have extended their reach so that programmes are available not only in a broadcast stream over the web but also for downloading over a seven-day period. Programmes made for TV screens are increasingly being viewed on the new screens by viewers with new-screen habits. TV programmes are just too powerful and lucrative as cultural items to stay within the confines of what used to be called television. New-screen viewers continue to use broadcast TV as a point of reference, but they search and access TV shows by name rather than by producers or broadcasters: they look for *Lost* rather than ABC, Sky One, Channel 4, Touchstone TV or Bad Robot. New-screen viewers look for content; TV viewers use channels, schedules and listings.

Yet, at the moment at least, it is that traditional form of television which continues to create the cultural and commercial value in those programmes. Broadcast TV is the launch pad for successful formats and the graveyard of those that fail to find an audience. Broadcast TV channels» have the production budgets to commission new formats, the know-how to mould the creative ideas into a form that suits them, and the marketing budgets to lure a sizeable part of the audience to try them out. They control the schedules which define new programmes by placing them at particular times on particular days. Broadcast TV is still the dominant force in the creation of television programmes. And, within broadcast TV, resources are

» Q37

Q2 What is 'television'?

still concentrated in a few channels. In 2005, the five UK terrestrial channels (BBC One, BBC Two, ITV1, Channel 4, Five) and their subsidiary channels provided sixty-two per cent of the total UK TV production investment of £4,692 million, despite providing just thirty-five per cent of the hours of original programming that were broadcast.[1]

Yet these broadcasters are haunted by the fear of their own demise, by the idea that their declining audience figures will continue to shrivel until no one will watch them apart from the old, the poor, the socially marginal and others of little interest to advertisers. Research appears to back this up, showing that a growing number of younger people have more developed new-screen viewing habits, and have little knowledge of or loyalty to traditional TV channels.[2] Today's teenager, it seems, is not lounging on the sofa waiting for the latest *Lost* or *The OC* to come on, but has already downloaded an illegal copy or has simply surfed for some plot information and derisive comments on the blogs and so is sufficiently authoritative about it without having wasted time watching it. As a result, broadcasters invest more in attracting this generation back to their screens, worrying that their medium is a thing of the past.

It is certainly true that TV viewing has lost its monopoly to new-screen activities. The total amount of TV viewed by individuals is slowly dwindling, but that is from a huge amount down to an awful lot. TV viewers are becoming more discriminating and less loyal to channels or to watching every episode of something they like, a trend that seems to have begun everywhere as soon as more than four channels became available. However, it is particularly dangerous to reach a conclusion about the inevitable decline of broadcast TV from examining the current behaviour of the young. New-screen viewing may be a particularly attractive option for that age group, whose social and physical mobility is great, whose tastes in entertainment are being formed, whose friendship groups are volatile and the source of much anxiety. The scheduled regularities of broadcast TV do not mesh very well with the spontaneity and changeability of the contemporary teenage lifestyle. Not for them is the normality of much of broadcast TV, though soaps provide a crucial means of self-understanding for many early teenagers, and particular TV shows can become cultural identifiers and 'must-sees' for many. They particularly relish things that they have discovered for themselves despite the mainstream media, like broadcasting. Nevertheless, it is often the case that this 'obscure' material may have been brought to their attention by major media corporations using techniques like viral marketing, or by deliberate launch on a more minority, obscure or teen-directed broadcast channel. However it may be that these must-sees come about, young people create social networks and a sense of communality through such common points of reference. This is startlingly similar to the process of sociality that most TV viewers also engage with through the shared experience of popular programmes. The regular parcelling out of time through the schedules of broadcast TV, however, seems to suit those with a more settled lifestyle. It remains to be seen, therefore, whether the new-screen habits of many teenagers will continue to dominate as their lives become more regular and crowded with commitments, or whether broadcast TV becomes a larger part of their post-teen style of life.

This is the crucial and unknowable question for those planning the future of broadcast TV. They know that the successful brands on new screens are very often those connected with their programmes, but they also know that their corporate identities are not well established on new screens, with the significant exception of the BBC. They know that currency is a key aspect of the appeal of their products both on TV screens and new screens. They know that, for the time being, they control access to the general social sense of currency, meaning that they are able to make a particular series into something that sufficient people (of the right sort for advertisers) feel that they need as well as want to watch. These viewers need to do so because the programmes provide a common point of reference, a means through which to belong to the same present as others.

Q2 What is 'television'?

Traditional broadcasters have one crucial advantage in the new-screen market: their editorial experience. Already many have evolved from organisations that made, marketed and showed programmes to ones that market and show programmes, many of which they have not produced. This involves a number of editorial functions, in both the selection of projects and collaborative (or sometimes confrontational) adaptation of those projects to the specific needs of their schedules. New-screen requires a further development of those editorial functions: to carry on a continual activity of selection on behalf of viewers from the explosion of material that is about to take place. A new-screen version of the BBC, CBS or Channel 4 would select and recommend material, probably organising it into streams that are suitable for particular times of the day or particular moods and uses. Such a new-screen 'content aggregator' would operate like a traditional television company but in a new-screen world. It would provide content that is time-tied and universal in its address, using many of the techniques of a push rather than pull approach. If its editorial approach were appealing enough, it would bring together audiences and satisfy the desire that television identified early in its history for a common sociality around entertainment. If the traditional broadcasters do not reinvent television in this way, then someone else certainly will.

Is there such a thing as 'good TV'?

There is good, bad and indifferent TV, just as there are good bad and indifferent meals. TV involves choosing which programmes to watch, and has done from the moment that competition between channels began. Yet there is little agreement about what a good TV programme is, or whether such a thing exists at all. Much TV watching comes into the category of guilty pleasures. We know that we should be watching an uplifting documentary or the news, but we would rather catch up with *Desperate Housewives* or the events on Ramsay Street.

Television's everydayness means that it consists more of consolatory entertainment, entertainment which provides comfort and release from the stresses of mundane living. It rarely claims more than this. The dimension of consolation stretches through mainstream entertainment, often called 'undemanding', like the cosy situation comedies *My Family*, *Fresh Prince of Bel-Air* and *Terry and June*, mystery drama like *Midsomer Murders* or *Murder She Wrote*, celebrity-based chat shows, game shows like *Who Wants to Be a Millionaire?*, lifestyle programmes like *Location, Location, Location, Dream Holiday Home* or *What Not to Wear*. A staple of consolatory entertainment, now almost totally disappeared, was the variety show like the *Billy Cotton Band Show* or *Sunday Night at the London Palladium*. Consolation is not without its raw edge, with the barbed comments of an Anne Robinson to contestants on *The Weakest Link* or the feelings of hubris generated by the sufferings of others on shows like *Wife Swap*, *Fat Camp* or *Brat Camp*. The sufferings of others, especially if self-inflicted, can be of great comfort to viewers averagely afflicted by the stresses of daily life. Consolatory entertainment goes over, renews and embellishes accepted beliefs about human nature. It shows us how well and how badly people can behave, tending to confirm what we already know. Its humour is funny because it calls on common experience and belief. It is not at all cutting edge, but it can be sharp. The knowledge it imparts is knowledge that fits with what we generally believe to be the case. This is an important but mundane function of TV, sometimes condemned as having a tranquillising effect in damping down legitimate feelings of discontent. But it equally serves to generalise the particular feelings and experiences of individuals as being part of a larger experience, whether it be a shared national experience or recognition of yourself (or of someone close) as 'that kind of person'. Consolatory entertainment has an important social role as it tends to be welcoming and inclusive, even to those who are ambivalent about some of its values. This is the key to the breadth of its appeal, but also of the sense of guilty pleasure which many feel whilst watching it. Presenters like Terry Wogan, Hughie Green, Bruce Forsythe, Cilla Black, Jonathan Ross or Graham Norton embody consolatory entertainment in their various ways. They are predictable and comfortable, and are able to appeal to a sense of humour and 'how life is' that has very wide resonances within the UK. Their gentle self-mockery blunts the barbs that are contained in their asides; their distinctive accents and tones confirm their positions as the licensed clowns of the electronic society. Consolatory television, whether clowning, variety or 'undemanding' drama, is often at odds with judgements about what constitutes 'good TV', even for those who enjoy it. Adults often watch it in a state of slightly guilty distraction. For younger audience members, learning the ways of storytelling and humanity, it is somewhat more compelling. But some of the programmes are truly awful, people say, even as they watch them.

The TV industry itself promotes three different and conflicting criteria of 'good television'. First there is simply the programme that is good within its own terms. There are good and bad chat shows, and more or less successful editions of each one. This judgement remains largely within the industry and is often confined to just the production team and the executives responsible for the series and channel. Reviewers seldom notice, as their time is largely taken up by the two other kinds of 'good television' as recognised by the industry. These are 'successful' programmes and 'quality' programmes. Successful programmes are largely defined by audience ratings, and can command greater resources, and a certain amount of indulgence for their foibles, as a result. Quality programmes are those which tend to call upon the values of quality in media other than television: documentaries that have an agenda and approach similar to that of the quality press; drama that relates to ideas of quality in literature and the film industry. It is rare to find a programme that is equally successful according to both standards. An example would be the BBC's serialisation of Dickens' *Bleak House* in 30-minute episodes over several weeks, which maintained a regular audience of around 5 million, about twenty-five per cent of the viewing audience. Normally, a quality drama will be slightly less successful in ratings terms than a long-running series with an eye-catching central conflict. In Europe, at least, quality drama is often equated with a relatively short series of four, six or eight episodes. The acknowledged

Q22

great works of television, the single dramas» and series written by Dennis Potter, David Mercer, Alan Plater or Stephen Poliakoff fall into this category of quality drama. Potter's work, whose best example is probably the series *The Singing Detective*, combines introspection with a social anger and a singular attention to the form of television itself. Poliakoff also directs his scripts in order to develop a sense of pace that is very different from that of almost all current TV drama. His BBC One series *The Lost Prince* was highly effective in bringing a large audience to an aesthetic of long scenes with little cutting. However, this kind of quality drama remains the work of individuals in the UK TV system. Longer series that attempt similar aesthetic innovations can be found at the HBO in the USA, which encourages the creative vision of a single artist working through large-scale production teams.

Even within the TV industry, which is based on the repetition of formats, repetition is seen as the enemy of quality. Many producers believe that to repeat a format is to exhaust it, both in terms of the writers' imaginations and the energy of the cast. Such an attitude is less marked in the US industry. Nevertheless, the rise of HBO series like *Six Feet Under*, *Sex and the City* and *The Sopranos* show that the US industry is also prone to judgments of quality

Q3 Is there such a thing as 'good TV'?

based on the idea of more filmic and/or literary qualities and an audience restricted to those who appreciate them. Yet for TV viewers it is clear that 'good TV' emphatically includes the familiar formats which become a part of people's everyday lives. *Dallas* and *Desperate Housewives*, *ER* and *Casualty*, *Big Brother* and *The X Factor* are 'good' because they are compelling. Their ongoing stories and character developments become personal and communal reference points during the period of their network exposure and first transmission. Anyone watching these series will be able to name their really good episodes: the one where *ER* told the story of Luka's car crash backwards; the fight in the Big Brother house and so on. These episodes are near to incomprehensible to someone who is not acquainted with the series to some degree. To understand Luka's reckless behaviour, we need to know his background, his back-story as a Croatian whose wife and children were killed in the Yugoslav civil war. To understand the *Big Brother* fight, we have to have seen not only some previous material from that series, but some of the press speculation about the individuals inside the house as well.

If judgements about good TV depend on being involved with it, then those judgements will tend to be temporary. Most TV is time-tied. A lot of programmes that were absolutely compelling when first transmitted seem inadequate or worn out after an interval of a decade **»** Q32, Q35 or two.**»** Seeing episodes of the BBC series *Compact* (1962–1965) again for instance made me recall what it was like to be entering my teenage years in the 1960s, bringing back all those awkward adolescent feelings of discomfort and embarrassment. Good or bad, *Compact* was important to me as a regular viewer. The same will be true for other people and other series. Much TV depends for the richness of its meanings on the current everyday moment of its transmission. And beyond a few genres like situation comedy, very few of the generally accepted classics of TV are easily available for people to see again. So what is 'good' tends to be a temporary, time-tied and personal assessment.

Occasionally, television brings forward a truly

exceptional event from the public sphere. As Dayan and Katz show, a series of public events in the second half of the twentieth century had television at their heart, from the assassination of President John Kennedy in 1963 to the public mourning of Diana, Princess of Wales after her death in a car accident in 1997. These are the 'I remember what I was doing when I heard' events, where the intimate and personal suddenly coincide with the public. Television is the meeting point between these two spheres, so plays a particularly important role in such events. They are 'good TV' in that TV is the forum in which the feelings of many are reflected back to them and validated. They are memorable TV because they remain moments where the everydayness of life was suspended on a national and even international scale. These remain exceptional events, and the more usual form of TV event is something that TV makes up for itself, like the relaunch of *Doctor Who* or the next run of *Big Brother*.

Judgements about good TV rely on an everyday involvement with TV, as much of its output consists of consolatory entertainment. Seen from the outside, from beyond the virtual community of viewers, most consolatory TV seems lame. So a significant amount of the public rhetoric about TV, and a good deal of conversation as well, condemns TV as a whole. Television provides a convenient target for newspaper commentators wanting to decry the decline of cultural and/or moral standards. Articles and people in conversation attack whole genres like reality TV rather than distinguish between particular examples of it. Outside the preview columns and listings pages, it is rare to come across a press discussion of TV which distinguishes between good and bad examples of a particular type of programme.

Does TV 'dumb us down'?

Television and dumbing down seem to go together. The term 'dumbing down' probably originated in the USA in the 1980s to describe a number of phenomena, including the declining standards in the formal education system, the collapse of established canons of accepted cultural value and the increasing value given to trivia. It became a useful term to describe any aspect of modern life that displeased the speaker or writer. Those who disagree argue that contemporary society requires different kinds of knowledge and intelligence from its citizens, and that the proponents of the notion of dumbing down are traditionalists whose values are becoming outmoded. This is essentially a new twist on an old debate which pitches an elite culture that sees its values under threat against a liberal view which finds fundamental values in popular culture.[3] Dumbing down remains a potent term, somehow

» Q11

evoking the image of a nation of obese couch potatoes**»** watching quiz shows or reality TV.

For proponents of the term, TV is a crucial part of the dumbing-down process. The reason for this belief lies in the fact that TV has been, from the start, a medium equally available to all. TV very quickly achieved a level of universality in the USA, UK and much of Europe after the end of the Second World War. In little more than a decade, it moved from technological miracle to everyday household object. It granted access to all kinds of knowledge and entertainment. It showed people things that they had never before seen, or even dreamed existed. But this sudden and general availability came at a cost. With few channels available, everyone was seeing the same material. This meant that it had to be calculated to be relatively inoffensive and, just as importantly, accessible to all. TV's extraordinary success meant the development of ways of speaking, ways of describing and packaging the world that assumed very little in the way of prior knowledge or skills. TV could not assume that the very diverse people who made up its audiences knew much about anything, so there could be no abstruse languages, no jargon (except jargon generated within television itself) and certainly no taking the attitude that 'you need to know that before you can know this'. Inevitably, the very universality of TV means that it is the prime target for accusations of dumbing down.

Universality has other costs. Though TV viewers as individuals all had specialist skills and knowledge, TV was unable to tap into them as it dealt with audiences in aggregates of millions. Compare this to the Internet, whose decentralised form means that anyone with Internet access can create a website. Here all and any language can be used; sites can be as abstruse or specialist as they please without censure. Indeed the use of technical languages adds to their usefulness to their core users, even if this means that there are many sites that offer the uninitiated no means of understanding what they are about. No problem: you just search for a definition of the technical term, or look for a more suitable site. No one complains about this aspect of the Internet, but they certainly would if such material appeared on television, as TV has been (and largely still is) a highly centralised medium. Television remains dominated by the size and diversity of its audiences. It remains a medium of the populariser, the specialist with the human appeal. TV operated in the realm of the ordinary person, or at least the person who appears ordinary, classless or demotic. Everything that is knowledge or information has to pass through this generalising process to make it accessible. This is not an easy process, and TV can often seem too simplistic. Certainly to watch a TV show about something you know and care about can be an intensely irritating experience. This is also the experience of finding yourself involved in an event that is picked up by TV news. Despite years of watching TV news and being able to mimic its rhetoric, the TV depiction of your event will inevitably be disappointing, ironing out its complexity and importance, and often losing the very thing that got you involved in it. Nevertheless, even people who have been through such an experience still tend to feel impatient with TV interviewees who seem unable to muster the necessary articulacy in front of the cameras. They are being interviewed to find out what we want or need to know from them, and not what they want to say.

Television is concerned with universal availability, so it brings sections of its vast audiences into contact with material that they have no interest in seeing. One aspect of the dumbing-down debate is an intolerance of the taste of others, especially of so-called 'low culture'. Television's universality brings all kinds of phenomena to the attention of people who would not otherwise come across them, like obscene language, laddish behaviour, crude and blasphemous jokes, soap-opera melodrama, *Big Brother* contestants and sport to name just a few. Television universalises popular culture just as much as it universalises knowledge about current events, natural history, poverty in Africa, the history of art and scientific principles.

As a result it seems to many people that popular culture has somehow become more pervasive and has edged out an older elite cultural values, so that the population as a whole has become dumbed down. This is true insofar as contemporary culture as a whole puts a greater value on the expression and understanding of emotions in both private and public life. Discourses of the emotions have become a part of everyday existence, and with them has come a need to examine the issue of whether extreme behaviour is either acceptable or excusable. Programmes like *Big Brother* are exploring many public values, not least the limits of acceptable interpersonal behaviour. The artificial environment of the contestants highlights the ways they try to relate whilst ensuring that they are not evicted, and how they try to relate in an environment stripped of the usual commodity supports. The show emphasises the differences between what is said to someone's face and behind their back to other people. The producers are constantly tempted to manipulate this (by revealing what is being said) to increase the tensions. Everyday

» 024

discussions of reality TV shows» tend to revolve around such questions, so these series are performing a valuable social function as a talking point, at least for those who are caught up in them. The format of the show is such that television viewers are either involved with its characters and progress or are left outside, puzzled or contemptuous of its evident tedium. As an early critic put it, 'Why not get them to redecorate the Big Brother house, then at least we would have the pleasure of watching paint dry.'

TV is open to the accusation that it is dumbing down precisely because it brings information and knowledge to the attention of people who would not otherwise have come across them. It can disseminate information to non-specialists (which usually annoys specialists), and it carries a lot of programming that is uninteresting or vaguely repellent to many people. This is an aspect of its role as a universally available, centrally organised form. The considerable editorial skills that underlie the scheduling» of such disparate material give broadcast channels» their distinct identities.

038
037

Q4 Does TV 'dumb us down'?

Does TV distort what it shows?

TV is frequently accused of distorting the situations that it shows. The presence of TV cameras tends to influence events, and some lament the fact that events of all kinds are staged to attract the attention of 'the media'. The presence of cameras is sometimes believed to inflame passions in tense stand-offs between police and demonstrators. It is still a relatively common belief that 'It wouldn't have happened if the cameras had not been there'. Whilst it

» Q10

is true that filming elicits performances,» it is impossible to separate public events in modern society from their portrayal, or potential portrayal, by TV. TV is now part of the everyday processes of life, and modern society without a TV presence within it is inconceivable. Society has become mediatised, and TV has been the crucial means of bringing about this new form of societal perception.

A mediatised society is a society that has augmented traditional forms of face-to-face and written communication with new forms of distanced audio-visual communication, and has changed how people interrelate as a result. In a mediatised society, citizens exist simultaneously in two spheres: the immediate, sensuous world of which they are physically a part, and a virtual world of knowledge, explanation and pleasure that comprises what is, somewhat inadequately, called 'the media'. Even an action as mundane as stepping onto a bus or going into a shop requires information derived from the media. It is equally accompanied by the media, through advertising, iPod use and the knowledge we bring in 'reading' passers-by from their clothes, gestures and speech. Roger Silverstone argued, developing Marshall McLuhan, that, 'like the natural environment, the media environment provides both the wherewithal, the resources, for the conduct of social life as well as the grounds of its very possibility.'[4] Media are not an optional add-on in a mediatised society: they are part of its very fabric, a constituent part of everyday experience, and a taken-for-granted part of existence.

TV is one medium among several which have brought

about the mediatisation of the modern world. The telephone and radio, the mass publishing of print and photos, and the cinema all became generally available half a century before TV, and between them they transformed person-to-person communication and provided a mass culture of words and images. TV, however, brought a new dimension: domestic and almost universal access to an ongoing stream of audio-visual material. It is the ubiquity and instantaneous nature of TV that has made it so key in the mediatisation of society. Television provides most people with their primary information about the world.**»** It remains the primary source of news about the wider world for the majority of people, despite the rise of Internet news sources (which are themselves often developed from the global TV news-gathering industry).[5] In the UK, sixty-eight per cent of people in 2005 named TV as their primary source of news about what is going on in the UK, and an even greater seventy-two per cent cited it as their primary source of news about global events. Even more remarkably, forty-six per cent named TV as their primary source of news about what is going on in their local area.[6] This second finding is particularly interesting, as the Ofcom annual survey has asked it regularly since 1995. TV has remained the primary source of local news, except in 2000–2001 when it was overtaken by newspapers. 'Talking to people' has declined from nine per cent to four per cent in the same period, rising higher only once, again in 2000–2001. This coincides with a crisis of trust in TV when the *Daily Mail* could carry the headline 'Can we believe anything we see on TV?'**»** The mediatised nature of modern society is clearly shown by the contrast between the proportion of people who use TV as the primary source of news about their local area rather than the people around them. It is even more remarkable since TV in the UK carries little local news.

The mediatisation of modern society has contributed to a growing feeling of the complexity of modern life. This feeling is evident in literary works that date from the very beginning of the process of mediatisation. Charles Dickens' *Bleak House*, which was sold as a serialised publication in

Q5 Does TV distort what it shows?

nineteen parts in 1852–1853, shows urban individuals caught in huge processes they cannot understand, involving subterranean and distant relationships. James Joyce renders the bewildering experience of urban life in *Ulysses*, including sections written in the languages of advertising and newspaper headlines. Both newspapers and radio, which was emerging as Joyce was writing, mediate distant events to individual citizens. The seeming complexity of modern life arises in part from this extended horizon of events which are occurring simultaneously but at a great distance. Awareness of global events brings people into a relationship with those events: they witness them through the media and thereby gain a sense of responsibility

» Q16

towards them.» Distant events belong to our time and so, by extension, belong to each individual who is aware of them. Radio, TV and Internet broadcasting mediate the increasing complexity of modern life, processing events into news, and views into public opinion. The broadcast media give form to the awareness of distant events even as they convey them: this is not so much a distortion as a necessary part of the process of creating awareness.

The profoundly mediated modern world requires both trust and responsibility, both of which are sometimes abused. What we know of the processes of the world comes primarily from media sources rather than from personal experience. Beyond our immediate world of personal experience extends another world: the world of public or general affairs with which we have continually to deal and which we know profoundly affects us. Misinformation can be easily spread through mass media like TV. It was possible for example for the US and British governments to claim that Saddam Hussein's regime possessed weapons of mass destruction, so justifying their invasion of Iraq in 2003. The UK's Joint Intelligence Committee reported that these weapons could be deployed within forty-five minutes, a claim that was used in a dossier of evidence before the invasion, which was quickly dubbed the 'dodgy dossier' by sections of the UK media. A similar claim was made by Colin Powell in a detailed speech to the United Nations on 5 February 2003. No such weapons have ever been found. Whilst some news sources were sceptical at the time, others, among them Fox News, continued to claim that Hussein's Iraq could mobilise weapons of mass destruction even after the invading troops had failed to find any. Fox News is often singled out as the main US news channel to do this, as it freely mixes right-wing opinion and news, despite its tag 'We report, you decide'. However, by 22 June 2006 – a mere three years after the invasion – even Fox News was debunking the claim by Senator Rick Santorum that weapons of mass destruction had after all been found in Iraq, claiming that it was a vote-winning ploy for the mid-term elections later that year.

This demonstrates two important aspects of the mediatised society. First, it is possible for governments and others to spread false information and to find news media that are all too willing to do so. But this also shows that good information will eventually drive out bad information. Fox News is a channel that tends to give its core audience what they want to hear, even if it involves a selective attitude to facts.[7] For Fox to debunk any 'proof' of Iraq's capabilities in 2003 demonstrates that there had been an important shift in information about the subject. Fox's previous editorial line had become untenable as good information had at last driven out bad. This, however, is of no comfort either to the inhabitants of Iraq or to the families of soldiers killed there. In a mediatised world, it is the present moment that matters, and the demonstration of connections between disparate parts of the world. The alarm around the 'forty-five minutes' claim shrewdly exploited both: the threat sounded both close and immediate, despite being neither of these. The misinformation achieved its aim in 2003 by justifying the invasion of Iraq. It also, perhaps, convinced key wavering politicians to support this much-disputed action. The corrections and revisions and, rarely, the apologies came a long time later.

TV is a pervasive medium, profoundly entangled with modern life. It is so much a part of modern society that it is unhelpful to see it as 'distorting' events. Instead, TV's specific role in shaping events should be examined in more

Q5 Does TV distort what it shows?

detail: how the sum of its coverage (or indeed the coverage by particular channels like Fox News) presents, interprets, hides or overemphasises. Along with dependence on TV for information comes suspicion of TV. A series of films, including *Network* and *The Truman Show*, reflect a widespread feeling that TV trivialises, reduces every event to a standard pattern and ignores some issues entirely. This suspicion of TV is a natural and healthy reaction to a dominant force in society and everyday life. Scepticism is a necessary state of mind in a democracy. It also means that TV and the people using it can never take it for granted that their messages will be trusted. Trust is not blind; it has to be won, and it has to be kept. TV always has to work to secure public trust, however much we as individuals may depend on it on a day-to-day basis for our information about the world.

Can we trust anything we see on TV?

The sounds and images available for us to view have multiplied exponentially in the past twenty years, and the question of which ones we can trust is becoming crucial.

Q37   Established TV channels» have built a relationship of trust with their viewers over a long period, and this relationship gives them an important place in the new-screen markets of the future. TV is unusual as a medium because it mixes factual and fictional output and so has evolved ways of making clear the distinctions between them. The makers of factual programmes claim to show the world 'as it is', and have to be trusted that this is indeed the case, but fiction has no such requirement. Trust has been central to broadcast TV because TV has constantly had to make clear the distinctions between fact and fiction in its output. The on-screen naming of programmes according to their genre type ('a documentary', 'the news', 'drama', 'comedy', etc) makes the distinction quite explicit and reinforces it. A constantly evolving set of rules shared by viewers and programme-makers has ensured that this key distinction continues to be generally understood. The distinction may seem simple, but there are many areas of overlap, from fictions based on fact and reconstructions of real events on the one side, to forms of reality TV that involve casting, scripting and shot-by-shot direction on the other.

Factual material can be defined as footage of events which took place in front of the camera with little or no direct guidance of the participants by the camera crew. It may well involve events which have been explicitly set up for cameras, like press conferences and photo calls, but in such cases it will be the participants rather than the TV crews who have organised them for the cameras. News material is the purest case of factual material. It involves the minimum level or near absence of intervention by the observing camera and its operators. News footage is also

Q15   recently produced. Within the current rhetoric of news,» those sequences or images that are used to provide a general context rather than to report are labelled 'library images' to indicate their non-news, though still factual, status. Graphics are used to provide explanations of scientific processes or technical economic issues, and these are obviously constructed within a studio reality.

The penalties for faking news footage can be severe. Michael Born worked as a freelance supplier to the RTL programme *Stern TV* and the Der Spiegel cable channel. Between 1991 and 1995, Born began first to reconstruct footage that he could not get legitimately and then to fake entire events. He used family and friends to do this, inventing clandestine activities like cat-hunting that would justify a degree of disguise. In an interview with an alleged 'cat-hunter', the man's fake moustache moves around his face as he talks. Even so, the *Stern TV* programme screened the footage as a news item. More ambitious items included child 'slaves' in India making carpets for Ikea. Born's undoing was to fake footage of a supposed German chapter of the Ku Klux Klan. This involved the display of Nazi insignia, which remains illegal in Germany. This triggered an investigation aiming to convict the alleged Ku Klux Klan members. Instead, it uncovered Born's serial faking of news items. He was convicted under German forgery laws in 1996 and was eventually imprisoned for four years. He remains unapologetic and claims to have faked about fifty such news items in total. He blames the lax editorial standards of the programmes he supplied, claiming both that he was incited to get increasingly sensationalist material and that his fakes were transparently obvious. This is certainly true of footage shown to US audiences in the CBS current affairs show *60 Minutes* about Born.

Born's case, his imprisonment and its coverage on primetime US TV all show the importance of maintaining the distinction between the fictional and the factual on TV. It matters because fact and fiction invoke different relationships to footage on the part of their viewers. Fictional material involves a 'willing suspension of disbelief';[8] factual footage involves an attitude of witness. News footage, and factual footage in general, calls on viewers to be witnesses to events. The TV cameras and their operators have seen the events themselves: their footage bears witness to those

TV FAQ

events. TV viewers are called upon to pay attention to that footage and to absorb its – often considerable – emotional impact.**»** This is a secondary act of witness, which still carries its own weight of involvement. We, the viewers, are given a sense of responsibility to the events that we see through television: having seen them, we cannot un-know them. Though we will not be called as witnesses in court (the footage itself, and perhaps those who shot it, will take care of that), nevertheless, factual footage still makes us witnesses. We know of the events; we have seen footage and have been able to inspect it as we now do all TV footage.**»** We know it to be a part of our shared world.**»** We may then think about our own situation and actions in relation to that knowledge, if necessary changing our attitudes and behaviour. In such circumstances, we need to be able to trust that what we are witnessing through television is factual in the terms that we understand. We need to know that our understanding of what constitutes factual footage is shared by those who shot the footage.

Fiction involves its viewers in a rather different network of assumptions. Fiction is still footage of events, of processes taking place, of people doing things, just as news footage is footage of events. But we trust that those events have a different status. When we view fiction, the assumptions that underpin our attitudes of viewing are different. Where factual footage brings us into a relationship of witness, fictional footage requires that we acknowledge that pretence is involved. Everyone in the process is pretending. Actors are pretending to be people they are not; writers are imagining and fantasising; directors and crews are mocking things up; and viewers pretend that it is not fiction whilst knowing that it is. We know that the events we are watching did not (and often could not) take place; nevertheless, we believe in them for the purposes of the fiction. The willing suspension of disbelief is a knowing pretence, a state deliberately entered into by viewers on the basis of trusting that everyone involved in the creation of the footage is playing the same game. The willing suspension of disbelief does not stretch to believing that the parallel world of fiction is the world that we inhabit.

Q6 Can we trust anything we see on TV?

The parallels are often compellingly strong, but they are still based on pretence.

There is, however, a considerable overlap between the production practices of fact and fiction, which is where the problems arise. Much fiction is grounded in thorough research so that its milieu is as plausible as possible, aiding the suspension of disbelief on the part of its viewers, and enabling them to relate the fictional world to their own. Much factual material is produced by a collaboration between film-makers and participants that is very different from the simple idea of a camera watching someone doing what they would be doing normally anyway. When we watch factual footage, whether it is documentary, interview or reality TV, it is frequently difficult to distinguish where performance ends and pretence begins. Everyone performs in a documentary, presenting a version of themselves for cameras and crews that they know to be present, and for audiences that they presume will be watching the resulting footage. Participants in documentaries and reality TV have agreed to appear to some significant extent, though **»** Q10 perhaps not in full awareness of what is involved.**»** Their **»** Q5 awareness of the cameras in our mediatised society**»** will bestow on them the role of performers, and it can be a totally sincere version of themselves that they perform.

Performance is not the same as pretence. Performance is the mode of self-presentation that people adopt in any interaction, and appearing on TV is simply another mode of interaction. Participants in factual TV are interacting both with those who are present (both within the action and those filming the action) and those who are not (the present or future viewers). Given that everyone involved is aware that this is the situation, people adopt particular forms of performance which are nevertheless a presentation of themselves. Pretence, however, is a different form of self-presentation, which involves deliberately taking on the appearance and behaviour of another, real or imagined. A significant part of the modern fascination with documentary on TV lies in trying to distinguish between the sincere performance of self and deceitful pretence. A documentary or reality TV participant who pretends to be other than they are is seen as betraying the trust that underlies the whole exchange. When non-celebrity Chantelle Houghton appeared on *Celebrity Big Brother* in 2005, it was made very clear to viewers that she was pretending to be a celebrity, whereas the other participant celebrities (assorted musicians, actors, notorious characters and politicians) were performing themselves. From the outset, Chantelle was required to convince the other participants that she was a member of a girl band in order to stay. Viewers were fully aware of her pretence. Her singing performance was relatively unconvincing but it nevertheless convinced the other celebrities, so she stayed on. Viewers generously voted her the winner, and she continues as a minor celebrity.**»** Chantelle Houghton's pretence was a known one, one that confirmed rather than broke the rules of factual TV.

Q24

The rules around the reality of news footage are strict, as Michael Born's case proves. Documentary material involves more intervention by its makers, and so the level of that intervention into the events is the subject of much debate. Born's footage resembles documentary closely: he clearly gave little guidance to his performers to increase the plausibility of what he was offering. Trust around documentary involves a delicate balance. Film-makers have to intervene considerably to set up even orthodox documentaries, negotiating for access to places, for permissions to shoot, for the agreement of potential participants, and at every stage they have to explain the nature and purpose of their programme. Once filming begins, everyone has a clear idea of what is expected. It has long been an occasional practice to ask a participant to repeat an action 'for the camera', because it was not captured well (or at all) when done 'for real'.[9] However, such forms of performance which shade into pretence occasionally cause real concern, irrupting into the realm of newspaper and general media debate. At such points, the underlying trust in the reality of factual footage can be imperilled. In 1999, the *Daily Mail* ran a series of stories about TV deception starting with the front-page headline 'Can we believe anything we see on TV?'[10] Clearly the

Q6 Can we trust anything we see on TV?

consensual trust in TV to abide by known rules was failing. At that time, reality TV was in its infancy, with the then novel form of the docusoap, which fused documentary and entertainment. It became clear that some series were going beyond the relatively acceptable practice of repeating actions, to the extent of proposing staged events and even of showing people in situations that were not their own. A series on traffic wardens, *The Clampers*, featured a boisterous warden who sang 'another one bites the dust' whenever he caught an illegal parker. It emerged that he was not an active warden; he once was, but had been promoted to a supervisory role some time before. He was asked by the producers to pretend to be an ordinary warden because he offered a more entertaining spectacle. Several other cases emerged, triggered by the discovery by *The Guardian* of an entirely faked documentary about the cocaine trade on ITV,[11] for which ITV was eventually fined £4 million. A general crisis of confidence in the trustworthiness of documentaries followed. Eventually, many individual film-makers and production companies resolved the crisis by altering popular documentary practice to make much more explicit any elements of pretence or prior arrangement. For example, many documentaries abandoned the idea of showing people going about their normal business, and **»** Q25 instead pitched them into unfamiliar situations.**»**

Most of the time, the consensual rules underlying the distinction between fact and fiction, performance and pretence are strong enough to allow a degree of comic or wild variation. The mock interview has become a staple of TV comedy. US shows like *The Daily Show with Jon Stewart* mix mild satire with spoofs on popular news forms, putting their inept reporters into invented situations. *Don't Watch That Watch This* goes further by re-editing and re-voicing footage of politicians to distort what they say. Chris Langham's creation Roy Mallard in *People Like Us* was simply a hopeless interviewer, adrift on a sea of irrelevant personal associations. Sasha Baron Cohen's creations Ali G and Borak confronted real interviewees (including major political or social figures) with an incompetent interviewer in an apparently real interview. Interviewees struggle with the interviewer's increasingly bizarre behaviour. Viewers are in on the joke; the interviewees are not. *The Mrs Merton Show* – featuring Caroline Aherne's fictional middle-aged 'ordinary' woman – and *The Kumars at No 42* – an indulgent British Asian family have built their son his own talk-show studio in the garden – present a more ambiguous form of comedy interview. Here the guests also know the artificiality of the situation, but the interview proceeds in a more serious vein. It can include genuine moments of revelation such as the late comic Bernard Manning's incomprehension at being accused of misogyny by 'Mrs Merton'. He seemed to have misunderstood the accusation as that of simply 'not being funny', and desperately appealed for support to fellow interviewee Richard Wilson (who played the grumpy old man Victor Meldrew, despite his leftish views). Wilson's visceral dislike of Manning's form of comedy came across vividly in his refusal to take Manning's side, and Manning began to brag about how much money he had made compared to Wilson. This was a case of reality breaking back through a spoof factual format.

Such comedy has a second function along with its ability to give immense pleasure. It confirms that we all – TV professionals, public figures and viewers alike – know the basic ground rules of truthfulness in contemporary television. It confirms that TV and its viewers are confident enough in the medium's ability to be trusted to adhere to them. These rules are continually changing as they adapt to new situations and the increasing sophistication of viewers. Trust has to be continually earned, and can break down under pressure of too much abuse.

Q6 Can we trust anything we see on TV?

Has TV changed politics?

TV has given a new visibility to politicians.[12] TV has brought politicians into the everyday world of people on TV, so their every expression and mood can be closely scrutinised. Few have met a prime minister, but everyone knows their voice and style of speech, their hairstyle, their grins and frowns, their particular gestures and involuntary body language. Most people will claim to be able to gauge their sincerity from these indicators, just as they do about people who appear in documentaries or reality shows. Some refer to prominent politicians by their first names only, as though they are actually acquainted, so close is the seeming link to these individuals through television.»

» Q14

The democratic political process has found it hard to adapt to the new visibility brought by TV. Radio broadcasting had proved to be a useful tool for traditional politics. In the 1920s, radio provided democratic politicians with a new platform, which they adapted to provide 'fireside chats' with their country, addressing citizens as individuals rather than as a mass in a public meeting. This was simply a new means of achieving an age-old need for those in power: to communicate their decisions to those they rule, and to secure their consent for those decisions. Broadcasting allowed rulers to speak directly and effectively. However, TV has brought a new personalisation of politics, reducing the traditional distance of national politicians from their people. Everyone now knows what their rulers look like and sound like. Impressionists have provided instantly recognisable lampoons of prime ministers since Willie Rushton's Harold Macmillan on *That Was the Week That Was* in 1962. Yet, just twenty years before that moment, it was possible to keep hidden from the American people that President Roosevelt was effectively confined to a wheelchair. Cinema newsreels and radio did not provide the same visibility that TV does.

TV gives us politicians in close-up. By appearing on TV, in broadcasts under their own control or on news or discussion programmes, politicians submit themselves to the same regime of understanding as any other TV performer. Their sincerity can be judged just like that of any other documentary or reality-show participant. This has thrown the emphasis of the political process onto the question of trust.» Now that the average citizen can see politicians daily and thinks they know them well, it is natural that they place more emphasis on a politician's personal characteristics than on the policies that they claim to represent. We ask not what policies they stand for so much as whether we can trust them to do the best for us. Politicians have responded in kind, proposing themselves as sincere and trustworthy when seeking election, and invoke the bond of trust that they believe they have created. Television enabled British citizens to see Prime Minister Tony Blair furrowing his brow and presenting his decision to join the US invasion of Iraq in 2003 as a struggle with his conscience. He explicitly appealed to the overwhelmingly sceptical British public to trust him. Many citizens (the majority according to opinion polls after the invasion had taken place) responded with the slogan 'not in my name'. This ruthlessly highlighted the inherent problem of representative democracy that has been intensified by the development of TV. Blair was appealing to the trust he thought he had won from the electorate. A majority responded that he did not represent their views on this important issue. It was an issue which no political programme or set of policies could have foreseen.

Television has exposed a problem at the heart of the process of democratic representation. Two principles of representation are involved: the idea of an individual whom you trust, and the idea of an individual who signs up to a set of ideas that you share. The process of democratic voting is one of picking an individual to represent your views and desires at governmental level. According to political theory, these individuals are elected as representatives of political programmes rather than as individuals. They represent a set of explicit aims (as do, e.g., the Greens) or a general tendency (as, e.g., New Labour). Under some democratic systems, citizens vote for lists of candidates rather than for an individual. Nonetheless, each list has its stars (who

Q7 Has TV changed politics?

feature at the top of the list and are likely to be elected), and its known individual leaders. In other systems, like in the UK and the USA, voting is for a particular individual as representative of a particular programme.

In either case, there is a double level of representation involved, and this introduces considerable ambiguity into the process: voting is for a person and a programme at the same time, and the two do not necessarily coincide. In the UK system, if a politician has a crisis of conscience and decides to join another party, they continue to represent the citizens of their constituency even though they were elected as the representative of a particular programme or party. Voters are given no chance, until another election is called, to revise their collective decision to choose that candidate. At that moment, the personal aspect of the contract comes to the fore. However, at other moments, the majority party will claim to have been elected on a programme including a number of unpopular measures. In seeking to push them through, they will claim that 'This is what the voters elected us to do', throwing the emphasis onto the principle that representation involves voting for a political project rather than an individual politician. At times, individual politicians themselves will vote against measures that were included in the programme on which they were elected.

The double system of representation (trusted person versus explicit programme) exists in an uneasy balance. Television has tipped this balance decisively towards the personal, by creating the feeling of a direct connection with individual politicians, usually the party leaders. Voting for a party programme has given way to voting for the appeal of a party's leader. That leader will propose a particular approach to politics rather than a concrete programme. They express themselves across their policy pronouncements and through them. Their programmes, such as they are, are more a vehicle for demonstrating their trustworthiness than they are a firm commitment to a particular course of action. Any politician putting forward a policy with less than total conviction is liable to be found out by the forensic viewing of voters,**»** so those policies still matter. Nevertheless, a shift has taken place in how the democratic process works, and democracies are still coming to terms with it. Democracy is beginning to work on the basis of a personal contract of trust between leaders and their citizens, but the system scarcely works well.

Modern politicians mobilise the idea of trust as the bedrock of their relationship with citizens. They will base their appeal on offering themselves as a trustworthy person, a person 'like you' or 'who you can do business with'. They appeal for the trust of the electorate on the basis of a show of sincerity, which viewers judge according to many other such appeals across TV. Politicians are then forced to present themselves as blameless in matters of personal morality in order to justify the trust of the electorate. In the prevailing morality of TV, trust requires that a person is open and sincere: to be caught being two-faced, duplicitous or hypocritical is one of the worst sins of reality TV.» However, politics is a process in which it is unwise to reveal everything that you hope for or intend to do, and this creates problems for many candidates. The area of personal morality is a further problem, as candidates usually want to present themselves as morally blameless rather than risk alienating part of the electorate. This provokes the inevitable investigations into their past or present acts of a dubious or unacceptable moral nature, and the spectacle of denigrating political commercials in the USA at election time. It is a rare politician who declares their past mistakes and uses this honesty as the basis of an appeal for trust. Rather, as with Bill Clinton and many others, the problems of their personal morality quickly become issues of trustworthiness, not so much because of what they did or did not do, but because they lied in order to cover it up.

The politics of seeming sincerity and trust involve a considerable amount of image management. Leaders are taught how to speak sincerely. This was famously the case with Margaret Thatcher, tapes of whose elocution lessons were widely circulated while she was Prime Minister, precisely to demonstrate that she lacked real sincerity.

Q7 Has TV changed politics?

All senior politicians calculate when, where and how they should appear, and employ teams of advisers whose role is to ensure that the some aspects of how they conduct their business remain hidden from their citizens. These image managers ensure that their charges continue to give an impression of sincerity and trustworthiness.

Sincerity is a performance for many politicians, not least because they are called upon to make many different kinds of pronouncements in different situations. In negotiations, sincerity is of little use, whereas other characteristics are: stubbornness, the ability to compromise, and the ability to imply something without actually saying it. Public political discourse still remains relatively formal in order to provide a flexible way of communicating on several levels at once, often by inference. Despite their seeming sincerity, politicians still use formal forms of speech most of the time. They frame their pronouncements carefully, even if they spice them increasingly with down-to-earth demotic phrases. Nevertheless, it is still a shock to hear how politicians speak to each other when they think the microphones are switched off. At a G8 conference in Russia in July 2006, President Bush and Tony Blair made the mistake of thinking they were. The conversation recorded was also widely broadcast to reveal the distance between their performance as public figures and how they speak in private. From Bush's greeting, 'Yo Blair', to Blair's reference to 'this trade thingy' and Bush's proposed solution to war in Lebanon ('what they need to do is to get Syria, to get Hezbollah to stop doing this shit and it's over'), the recording revealed a discourse somewhat less elevated than the average daytime chat show, let alone a current affairs programme. It equally showed the hesitant and craven attitude of Blair to Bush, through both his speech and his body language, standing whilst Bush sits munching a sandwich.

Such glimpses of the actual interaction of politicians reveal how little we really know them. Our politicians are visible to us, but they still largely control the terms of that visibility; they determine when and how they are seen. TV may have enabled a visibility and brought a new relationship of familiarity with politicians. But this relationship can still be controlled and manipulated. It also carries with it a danger of disillusion with the political process itself, especially if attempts to manipulate the relationship begin to go wrong. TV has introduced an 'up close 'n' personal' approach to politicians which has intensified the representational contract by enabling citizens to make a judgement about the sincerity of politicians and whether they are 'sympathetic'. In this new political landscape, disappointment and disillusion with a once-trusted politician are frequent phenomena. This can contribute to a disillusion with the whole process of politics and the negotiation of collective endeavour. The show of sincerity and the appeal for trust are easily abused. The resultant disillusion can be felt more keenly as a personal betrayal than, for example, the attempts by politicians in the past to abandon or revise a central plank of policy. Disillusion with politics, in other words, may not be the result of an increasing distance from those in power at all. It seems more to be the result of the feelings of closeness to politicians that TV has brought about, and the subsequent disappointment when that personal relationship is betrayed.

Is TV rubbish?

One of the most general complaints about TV is that most if not all of it is 'rubbish'. This is indeed true, but only if rubbish is the discarded once-important stuff of everyday existence. Rubbish is what remains after something has been consumed, like food wrappings and leftovers. Rubbish is material that was once important but has since lost its importance. Last week's news and last month's breakfast chat show, last year's editions of soaps and sports events from even a few weeks back are at best nostalgic relics to the viewers who were once eager to see them, perhaps to the point of arranging their day to make it possible. TV is an everyday medium, used and then discarded. TV programmes are a part of the texture of everyday life. They are scheduled to appear at the same time each day or week in a regular pattern that echoes the patterns of everyday life for most people. One characteristic of the everyday is its repetition of the same basic patterns and timings of getting up, going to work, eating, going to bed. Television schedules consciously respond to these patterns, providing different kinds of programming suited to the different 'day-parts' as they are known in the industry.

》 38 Television is moulded to, and moulds, everyday life.**》**

It sits in our living spaces, with 25.3 million homes in the UK having at least one TV in 2005. This is virtually all the households in the country, which had a population of around 59.6 million in 2003. In the UK, forty-four per cent of households have three sets or more, including twelve per cent with a set in the kitchen. Virtually everyone watches them too, with ninety-five per cent of the British population watching TV in any one week.[13] In the USA in 2006, Nielsen Media Research estimates that there were 111,348,110 households with TV sets (an increase of 326,719 on 2005). A top-rated network show like *Desperate Housewives*, *Gray's Anatomy* or *NBC Sunday Night Football* is seen by twenty to twenty-two million people on its first run, meaning that over ten per cent of the adult population are watching the same show on the same channel. TV characters

TV FAQ

can become almost as familiar as family members. TV has worked on increasing this effect. The decline of single dramas and documentaries in favour of series, a long-term trend in European TV, is the result of television taking its place at the heart of everyday life. We are familiar with a large group of magazine programme presenters, lead characters in fictional series and individuals in factual series who return week after week. Many of the actors move from one format to another, but play essentially the same person, like David Jason in the UK and David Caruso in the USA. This familiarity is a key part of the everydayness of television, but with this familiarity always comes something novel: the new situation, the new story, the new challenge for our familiar characters.»

30

TV is not just another familiar household item. It brings extra dimensions into the everyday life of households: the dimension of the public as well as the dimension of fiction. If it behaved just like another member of the family, it would appeal only to those deprived of everyday domestic human contact. TV brings in the outside world, the world of other people in all their difference from us; the world of politics and public events over which we have no real control. It brings things we would rather not watch or know about, as well as things which give immense pleasure. It also brings a sense that we individuals in front of their screens are not alone. We are watching what other people are watching. TV programmes provide easy subjects for conversation and sharing. TV channels work by creating a sense of togetherness in separation, by using what Paddy Scannell defined as a 'for anyone as someone' structure.[14] All the voices of TV – its presenters, its factual commentators, its continuity announcers – use particular forms of language which give an individual viewer the feeling that they are being spoken to as an individual. But at the same time this address is consciously universalised as much as possible. The language habitually refers to the present moment, the shared moment of reception, using terms like 'now', 'here', 'we' and 'you', all of which depend on a shared context for their meaning. In this way, television mediates the public world of events and

Q8 Is TV rubbish?

issues into the private and domestic world of individuals. It puts the public in personal terms, dramatises issues into individual stories, and stolidly asserts the ordinary in the face of the extraordinary.

This is TV's strength but also its undoing. The executives responsible for TV output have a difficult balancing act to perform between the two contradictory pulls of TV. One is its familiar and mundane domestic aspect, and the other its ability to uncover the exceptional, the new and the unacceptable.**»** TV brings the exceptional into the space of the everyday, literally because it is watched in the space of everyone's homes. TV is often seen as a meretricious medium, as rubbish, simply because it is an everyday medium. In western culture, the everyday has been regarded as unimportant precisely because it happens every day, as does television. Western culture has traditionally made a series of distinctions between the mundane and the exceptional. Historically, everyday life has been seen as the grind of existence, the tedious business of struggling to stay alive, which is lightened by special moments of joy, of deep or transcendental feeling. This is a fundamental aspect of much religious and philosophical thought. Some more ascetic trends seek to liberate the chosen few from the trammels of the everyday, whether they are monks, celebrities or academics who seek to escape from 'administration'. All require 'someone else' to do the mundane things, so that they can concentrate on the 'more important'. Other more puritanical trends emphasise the importance of the grind of the everyday as the gateway to the sublime. For this tendency, the road to enlightenment involves hard work and mutual support. Measured by this standard, too, TV falls short because the medium is deceptively simple to watch and enjoy. It seems to involve no effort on the part of its audience, unlike other forms of culture which require a work of initiation before they can be enjoyed.[15] Both variants of this view, which is deeply ingrained in western culture, make the same basic distinction: everyday life is less important than the exceptional or the transcendent. Such attitudes lie behind the accusation that TV as a medium is rubbish. It

» Q4, Q40

is intimately a part of the everyday, and since everyday life has traditionally been seen as trivial or unimportant, then so must TV be valueless.

Consumer society has blurred such distinctions by making everyday life more acceptable and more comfortable for the majority in the western world. Some of the tedium of everyday tasks has been reduced by the use of domestic appliances and new materials for clothing. And many routine tasks have been invested with an amount of glamour, and a promise of passing pleasure. TV advertising (and programming) has been a powerful contributor to this process. Contemporary consumerism tries to heighten the everyday activities of consumption, and to invest them with a trace of the transcendental. Comedy sketches about advertising have seized on this, exaggerating the disparity between a humble product like a shower gel and the orgasmic response of the female user presented in the TV commercial. Advertising, quick to appropriate any idea, responds with its own self-mockery that amazingly still maintains the essential premise: that there is pleasure or at least satisfaction to be had from the mundane activities of everyday life. The advertising promise has become slightly defensive and apologetic. Recent advertising seems to be saying, 'Yes, we know that shower gel won't really get you going to this extent, but just think about it for a moment... you can shower in a more comforting way, in a more, well, enjoyable way if you use our product.' The promise has the effect of continuing to confirm, despite the irony, that there is something significant about everyday life.

TV is denigrated as a medium because it is everyday and domestic, and mediates the exceptional to the mundane. This is an important social function rather than a reprehensible activity. But it does not mean by any means that everything that TV does is good. There is good TV and bad TV, and there is plain stupid TV. There is memorable TV and eminently forgettable TV, just as some ordinary days are better than others. A lot of TV is consolatory entertainment which by definition is comforting rather than challenging, and is enjoyed rather guiltily.**》** However, there are hours of TV material that

》 Q3

Q8 Is TV rubbish?

seem to exist simply to keep the adverts apart. It is one thing to claim that TV as a whole is not rubbish; quite another to claim that there is no rubbish on TV. There are plenty of badly conceived formats like the tedium of ITV's *Celebrity Love Island* or mawkishness of ITV's *Fortune: Million Pound Giveaway*. These are programmes that many prefer to forget even whilst watching them.

Is TV an agent of globalisation?

TV has enabled us to see the world from the outside. This was quite literally the case with the pictures of the globe sent back by astronauts in the 1960s. Apollo 8 in 1968 showed the Earth from the surface of the Moon; by July 1969 a huge audience was gathered through TV, estimated at 600 million people worldwide,[16] to see images not only of men on the Moon, but also of the Earth seen as a planet in space. The image of the Earth as a cloudy ball became one of the iconic photographs of the following decade, and one of the most reproduced.

This was the defining moment in TV's process of showing people back to themselves as others. This was the othering of the entire planet, offering a perception of the shared physical limits of human existence. It defined the planet as an entity, helping to spread the perception of the Earth as a single ecosystem. It inaugurated a conception of multiple worlds within one world, of a sense of the boundedness and interconnection of life on the surface of this one planet. From this moment, it was less easy to perceive the world as multiple and endless, where there were places left to explore and to exploit. Gradually, the idea of multiple 'worlds' gave way to the dominating notion of one single world which is shared by all the people who live on it. This helped the development of a popular concern with the fragility of our planet.**»**

At the same time, TV has made its viewers aware of the sheer diversity of humankind. More than any other medium, TV has made people aware of the otherness of other people. Through a wide range of TV programmes from sitcom to documentary, versions of the private lives of others have been put on display. The smallest eccentricities become the subject of sitcom episodes. People's strange ideas of interior decoration, their bizarre hobbies and obsessions are revealed in home and personal makeover shows like *How Clean is Your House?* and *Clean Sweep*. Unreasonable behaviour, strange parenting practices and disturbing family interactions are seen in programmes like

Q45

Brat Camp, House of Tiny Tearaways, and *Wife Swap.* We are able to see into the intimate spaces of others, and to share their secrets as they try to reform themselves.**»** The otherness of other people is routinely on display through such programmes: the strangeness of those who live in the next street or town, and the diversity of those who live in far-flung places and radically different cultures. Reality TV convinces its audience of the eccentricity if not insanity of fellow citizens just as much as it does their shared characteristics.**»** TV news brings us the suffering of others and the incomprehensibility of others in equal measure.**»** News subsists on a diet of catastrophe, of war and famine, terror and repression, natural and man-made disaster. Less often does news bring the everyday life of those distant others, their moments of happiness and boredom, of sympathy and humour. This is more the work of documentary and of fiction, which can develop insight into individuals and their motivations, and show the life of other cultures from the inside. Nevertheless, it is the case that, in most western countries, the news happens every night, but such insightful dramas or documentaries are rarer. Documentary and fiction tend to concentrate on people more like us or closer to home, so there is only a limited possibility that news awareness of the lives of distant others will develop into a deeper empathy.

TV has brought an awareness of difference as well as an awareness of a fundamental communality. It shows us seemingly incomprehensible people and actions on the face of a globe that it has demonstrated to be shared and finite. This is one of the great paradoxes of modern times, creating what sometimes seems an inevitable tendency towards intolerance and isolationism. In fact, it is not so much a paradox as a process. TV does not show unified versions of the world but fragmented perceptions of it. News is particularly fragmented.**»** TV is also a greedy medium, running in multiple channels for twenty-four hours every day, it is an industry that seeks out cheap material to fill space. Much of this is imported from other cultures, bringing other cultures into the flow of TV.**»** Some commentators rightly emphasise that most viewers see much of one particular kind of other culture, that of the USA. Some went even further and predicted a globalisation of TV culture dominated by US material. However, something far more interesting and complex has happened instead. The trade in programmes has developed to embrace more cultures, and the reception of those imported programmes has created what may evolve into a form of global citizenship.

Those who predicted the rise of a global TV culture dominated by Hollywood products tended to overlook other cultures with thriving TV exports. These include the export of Mexican and Brazilian telenovelas throughout and beyond the Hispanic world, including to the Spanish-speaking citizens of the USA. Within Europe, there has long been a widespread trade in programmes, with Britain occupying a further role in the world market as the provider of an elusive 'quality' that seemed to elude Hollywood TV, at least until the rise of HBO. Australia exports to the USA; South Korea to China and Japan; Egypt and Lebanon to the whole of the Middle East. Satellite and Internet channels further add to the availability of programming from beyond national boundaries.

Where imports have arrived into a national TV culture, they have had a particular kind of reception. They are recognisably distinct from the local programming. They often have superior production values;**»** they show worlds that are sometimes completely alien yet provide characters and dilemmas which engage the imagination and sympathies of many viewers. Imported programmes become a particular genre, an addition to the range of TV rather than a direct alternative to local productions. It is often the case that, though they have inferior production values, local programmes nevertheless attract larger audiences than imports. They are usually based on the cultural specifics of one place or nation: the intricacies of taste, accent and turns of phrase that allow people to recognise themselves as part of a common 'us'. They include stars and jokes, places and concerns that would meet with blank incomprehension from anyone outside that culture. Any Briton who has tried to explain the appeal of Graham

Q9 Is TV an agent of globalisation?

Norton or Peter Kay to someone from outside the UK will know what cultural specificity is about.

Yet audiences do recognise something of themselves in imported programmes, despite the manifest cultural differences. They provide a link with a wider – world – culture which is distinct from any national cultures. In effect, TV has begun to produce at least a dual cultural identity within its viewers. They participate in a local or national sense of being 'part of ourselves', but also have another identity as part of a global communality that embraces the shared experience of popular imports from *Dallas* to *Monty Python*. Yet, equally, research has shown that each TV culture that imports these programmes makes them their own. People mould what is offered by international TV culture to their own needs and preoccupations. Liebes and Katz, for example, found that some Israeli viewers of the widely exported US primetime soap *Dallas* apparently regarded it as a criticism of the extravagant capitalist values that American and European viewers thought that it endorsed. Through their study of different audience groups in Israel, they found that some Russian Jews discerned a self-criticism of capitalism, and some Arab viewers watched it as an example of the decadence of western culture along the lines of the critique offered by the Muslim Brotherhood.[17] Such varieties of interpretation are less than surprising, but are often overlooked in critiques of the globalising tendencies of television. Global TV culture exists everywhere only in its local variants. Global TV is no different from the increasingly global language of English in this respect. Chinese English, American English, Indian English, Nigerian English, Australian English, Filipino English and English English are distinct and different versions of a flexible language, moulded by the rhetorical traditions and local needs of the culture that is using it. International exchanges increasingly require an understanding of those traditions even when the superficially shared language called 'English' is being spoken. The TV programmes that circulate internationally are subject to the same uses.

This spread of English as a global language with many

local adaptations reveals a third factor in globalisation. The conflict and negotiation between the local and the global goes along with the increase in cultural diasporas and interchanges. Sizeable groups of people from radically different cultures now inhabit the cities of the world and many have done so since well before the development of TV as a mass medium. Those groups who settled during the twentieth century have been able to bring elements of their own cultures and religions with them and have stayed in touch with those cultures. Many of the estimated 760,000 British people living in Spain[18] use UK television and maintain a parallel existence that has little interaction with the Spanish culture surrounding them. Assimilation to the host culture has become less of an imperative for many diasporic groups, as is demonstrated by the growth of a Spanish-speaking community in the USA, the first major group to settle in that country and maintain its own language. The growth of easily available mass media has increasingly enabled a trade in films and TV programmes from 'back home'. The rise of the VCR (video cassette recorder) in the late 1970s brought London a substantial inflow of films from India and Hong Kong. As TV channels diversified, Zee TV was launched in 1995 and now has additional music and film channels, and PTV Prime became a free channel on the Sky menu in 2006. These channels engage in production for their target audience, and this production draws on a growing use of low-cost video and Internet communications. This is a familiar pattern in many countries and it complicates the distinction between the global and the local. It also provides a visible presence of other cultures in the world's major cities, and those cultures are becoming more articulate. As multiple cultures articulate their desires and identities within the same spaces, there is some fruitful exchange and some real tension. Mainstream TV comedy can be one of the means of negotiating that tension, through rare series like *Goodness Gracious Me*.

The globalisation of TV has not brought an unstoppable tide of Hollywood TV to the screens of the world, although many of the formats and habits developed in Hollywood have become standard across the world's TV cultures. Some aspects of American consumerism have been spread by US TV (and cinema) but have been subtly altered in the process. Globalisation has tended to create new supplementary cultural identities rather than destroying local or indigenous cultures. It provides the necessary starting point for a global understanding. It does not itself provide that understanding, or anything close to an understanding. But TV has helped to bring about a degree of realisation that the world is a common space, occupied differently but fundamentally shared. For those that choose to look, global axes of power are relatively clear, as is the otherness of the other people who occupy the planet. As dealt with by TV, this realisation is neither a comfortable one, nor an analytic one. It has taken the world to a new kind of volatility.

Does TV exploit people?

The charge that TV exploits people is almost as old as the TV documentary itself. Documentaries involve revelation, and the more that documentaries are concerned with emotions, the more that they stand accused of exploiting those who appear in them. The acceptable levels of self-revelation differ from country to country and time to time. So British audiences tend to find the level of exhibitionism of *The Jerry Springer Show* somewhat uncomfortable, but those same audiences tolerate a degree of televisual nudity that would be unacceptable in factual programmes in the USA.

The key to exploitation is the level of informed consent. Anyone appearing on TV has to know what they are getting themselves into. However, this is more easily said than done, as the impact of a new TV format – like *Big Brother* for its first contestants – is impossible for anyone to gauge. And it is simply impossible for anyone who has not experienced the presence of cameras in their lives to judge what impact they might have. Even in a society permeated by cameras, where most people are used to how they appear in moving images from home videos or mobile phone footage, the impact of something made explicitly for a wide audience of strangers – which is what TV is about**»** – is still hard to judge for anyone outside the TV industry. The level of glamour or flattery involved in the possibility of being seen by those strangers has a heady effect. So however informed the consent of individuals in documentary or reality TV may be, there can still be some doubt about whether they knew what would happen to them.[19] Few people have the self-awareness to know how they will really appear to others, and producers know that those with limited self-awareness – or massive self-delusion – often make the best subjects.

Several stories illustrate the problems of consent. On rare occasions, the lack of informed consent can be justified because the programme was made for 'the greater good', that the revelation for the majority was worth the violation of an individual's in principle right not to be exploited. This is the case for Paul Watson's films about the extremities of old age, *The Home* (where interviewees were clearly beyond the realm of informed consent) or *Malcolm and Barbara… A Love Story* (1999), with its portrayal of advanced Alzheimer's disease. However, many situations are less clear-cut.

Sometimes participants are deliberately not made fully aware of the nature of the programme in which they had been invited to participate. When Jonathan Schmitz participated in the recording of a *Jenny Jones Show* made by Warner Bros for NBC in 1995, he was simply told that it would reveal a 'secret admirer'. When the show was taped, in front of a studio audience, the secret admirer was revealed as another man, Scott Amedure. Amedure described his fantasy about Schmitz involving whipped cream, strawberries and champagne. Schmitz was outraged; indeed, he was so outraged and ashamed that three days later he sought out Amedure and shot and killed him. Amongst the evidence at his trial was a note from a programme researcher to Jenny Jones stating that Schmitz hoped that his crush was a woman. It then said 'Scott [Amedure] has an inkling that Jon [Schmitz] is bisexual' and that Jon is 'going to die when he sees it's Scott'.[20] Schmitz was eventually sentenced to twenty-five to fifty years' imprisonment for murder. At the trial it was argued that Schmitz knew there was a possibility that he would be embarrassed during the show. Nevertheless, it seems that his homophobia, lethal in this case, was not something that had been sufficiently explored by the programme researchers. They had been more concerned with how visibly embarrassed Schmitz would be when the unexpected nature of his admirer was revealed. They would have lost this moment of emotional display if Schmitz had known what to expect.

My second example concerns an early Channel 4 experiment in what is now known as reality TV. In 1992, a programme was made for the Valentine's Day-themed *Love Weekend*, which followed people who were still virgins despite their advancing years. The concept involved providing them with a number of dates to see how they fared. At the press launch – held rather unadvisedly on a riverboat travelling down the Thames – a journalist interviewed one of the male participants, someone who was presented as a social marginal, a friendless individual. Asked how he had enjoyed the experience of making the programme, he said it had changed his life because he had gained a new best friend. It was not obvious from the programme which of his dates this might be, so the journalist delved further. 'Oh, it's the director of course. He's so interesting to talk to,' was the reply. A recurring problem for documentary directors is that they tend to get involved with their subjects. However, this shows how such a relationship can be exploited. It is more than likely that the individual concerned found that his new best friend cooled rather rapidly once the programme had been safely broadcast.

My third example is the series that eventually became *Family Therapy* (BBC Two, 1995). This groundbreaking series aimed to put the actual process of therapy on-screen for the first time. It was produced by the late Udi Eichler, himself a trained psychotherapist. A number of other therapists were also involved in screening the volunteer family to ensure that they would not just endure but actually benefit from the triple process of therapy, being filmed and subsequent public scrutiny. Eventually a suitable family was found, and they embarked on the process of therapy and the filming of it. After five weeks, it was revealed that the father of the family was abusing one of the children. The filming was immediately ended, and the eventual series was made by a different method, and featuring another family entirely. In the case of this abortive filming, the abusing father was, as abusers often do, using the filming to raise the stakes in relation to his own feelings of power and guilt. This was an abuser relishing his own invincibility. He believed he could fool the whole world. This feeling was only confirmed for him by the range of experts who screened him and failed to discover his secret.

These three cases show the difficulties involved in

obtaining revealing factual material whilst ensuring that informed consent exists. As the *Family Therapy* example demonstrates, the motives of those volunteering to appear in documentaries can be as dubious as those of the programme-makers. Schmitz's tragic example shows that fully informed consent can be incompatible with obtaining the desired material. Any TV appearance will flatter those who appear. The predominant motive for those who appear is not so much fifteen minutes of fame in front of strangers as a more sustained period of attention from the programme producers. The Valentine's Day programme may be an extreme example, but it is still rare even in a society of therapeutic discourses to be given the feeling that your emotions and dilemmas are of compelling interest to others. This is not to say that those who appear in documentaries and reality shows are attention seekers, though some definitely are. It is more to show how the behind-the-scenes aspects of factual programme-making are of key importance, with programme-making teams making potential interviewees feel as though they are the centre of attention. This is carried through into the act of filming itself, where an interviewee's utterances can be heard in a respectful silence (for the purposes of 'clean' sound) – a rare occurrence in real life. For many, it is equally rare an experience to be asked questions in a sympathetic and interested manner, as directors or interviewers routinely do.

The exceptional nature of the filming process results in the common feeling amongst disgruntled programme participants that they were in some way misled about the intentions of the show on which they appeared. It also results in the common accusation that documentaries exploit people by putting them into a situation that distorts their normal behaviours. They perform a version of themselves as everyone performs a persona in situations involving strangers. But in the case of factual TV, they are flattered into a belief in their own importance, and this can lead to a kind of exploitation. With the development of more intrusive filming technologies, this question of exploitation has become an issue of more general public concern. The development of new formats of reality TV can be seen as a response to this concern. Shows like *Wife Swap*, *Brat Camp* and even *Big Brother* provide an explicit level of competition or challenge that deliberately take participants out of their everyday lives.**»** In this way, some of the problems of informed consent are suspended, as the participants are being invited to adopt a persona or try out performing as someone other than their self-image. It remains for viewers to try to glimpse the 'real person' behind the mask adopted for the show.

Does TV make you fat?

On the face of it, TV has made couch potatoes of us all. According to Ofcom's survey of UK audiences in the year 2003, twenty-four per cent of respondents said that they watched between two and three hours a day, another thirty-three per cent said they watched between three and five hours, and ten per cent watched more than seven hours each day. Surprisingly perhaps this last category contained far more pensioners than teenagers, with nineteen per cent of over-65s saying they watched more than seven hours a day against seven per cent of 16–24-year-olds. Eighty-seven per cent of those questioned said they watched every day, and that was pretty consistent for all age groups, with just one per cent saying they watched less than once a week. Four-fifths of households have more than one TV.[21] So the couch-potato effect might seem to be irrefutable, apart from the fact that it seems to be pensioners rather than teenagers who are stretched out on the sofa watching any old stuff.

But it all depends on how this TV watching is done. The term 'couch potato' invokes the image of one particular kind of viewing, that of a mesmerised, obese person staring at a screen that provides the only illumination in the room. The image is familiar from films and TV commercials but less, it would seem, from real life. There will be such morbid TV viewers out there, but TV viewing is more often conducted along with other activities, except in the case of particularly complex or affecting material like major drama or breaking news.

At least that is what can be deduced from personal observation. The topic has been little researched, as the majority of surveys into TV viewing divide into two categories. First there are those that are keen to link TV viewing with various ills in society, from violent behaviour to obesity. These tend to be paid for by government, health agencies or charities. The TV industry and marketing more generally are interested in media usage only, » so very few holistic studies are carried out into TV viewing. They are

» Q39

both expensive and difficult to complete: the most famous, by Peter Collett at the beginning of the 1980s, installed video cameras inside TV sets to observe consenting British families whilst they watched. The footage proved impossibly huge for the research team to analyse properly, and little has been published from the study,[22] but it did provide some revealing material for the TV series *Open the Box* (Channel 4, 1986). TV sets were on for long periods with no one watching. When there were viewers present, they were often talking, eating, cutting each other's hair, practising musical instruments, doing homework, reading, exercising, sleeping or becoming intimate. The footage revealed the sheer variety of activity that took place, and the low attention paid to the screen for much of the time. This study has not been followed up in the intervening years, mainly because of the degree of intimate exposure of people's private lives that it involved.

Collett's study was carried out in an era when TV was still dominated by a few network channels and the VHS recorder was a comparative rarity. Contemporary studies from the TV and marketing industries do tend to confirm that TV viewing is commonly combined with other activities. The US market research organisation Knowledge Networks reckoned in December 2004 that 'The proportion of viewers doing other things, such as talking, snacking or reading while watching primetime TV, has increased slightly since 1994, from 67% to 75%.'[23] A more wide-ranging study into simultaneous time use, sampling 13,414 Americans, unfortunately confines itself to the question of whether people are using different media at the same time. Nevertheless, its results are startling. Three-quarters (74.2 per cent) said they regularly or occasionally watch TV and read the newspaper at the same time, and 66.2 per cent are regularly or occasionally online whilst watching TV, with up to a third doing this regularly. Two-thirds (66.3 per cent) read their mail whilst watching, and this rises to 80.7 per cent in that hard-pressed group whose PDAs run their lives. These figures generally show an increase on the previous year. Another study of Americans between the ages of eight and eighteen showed that media multi-

Q11 Does TV make you fat?

tasking is increasing, with young people exposed to media for eight and a half hours a day, and spending twenty-six per cent of that time 'multi-tasking' – using television, videos, music, video games and computers at the same time, often while doing homework.[24] The image of the teenager is someone with TV and radio or other music media in the background, doing homework by texting friends and – unfortunately for their teachers – cutting and pasting from the Internet.

Not all viewers are this active, however. Another group of surveys has highlighted the problem of combining TV watching with eating. A well-publicised piece of research by a group of American doctors into female obesity deduced that, from their sample of 50,227 women between 1992 and 1997, 'time spent watching TV was positively associated with risk of obesity and Type Two diabetes. In the multivariate analyses adjusting for age, smoking, exercise levels, dietary factors, and other covariates, each two hours a day increment in TV watching was associated with a 23% increase in obesity and a 14% increase in risk of diabetes'.[25] Popular sources of medical 'knowledge' explain this by attributing it to excessive eating whilst watching TV or to physical inactivity: 'People who watch a lot of TV also happen to do [the] least amount of exercise – couch potatoes', according to holistic-online.[26] This website helpfully explains this in simple terms that may or may not accord with how real humans work: '[The] trance-like effect that is created by TV-watching leaves the brain thinking it needs something and, not knowing exactly what it wants, it decides that food is the easiest answer.' Interestingly, it is quite possible to watch TV and exercise. In gyms this is exactly what occupies (and isolates) all those people pedalling stationary cycles or running on the spot. No survey seems to have tried to find out how many people do this at home.

There is certainly a link between large amounts of TV watching and obesity, but it is by no means necessarily a causal link. For adults, watching TV for many hours a day is itself often a symptom of deeper problems like loneliness, boredom and feelings of rejection, which are

TV FAQ

often themselves linked to excessive eating, self-neglect and lack of exercise. Excessive TV viewing, in other words, may well be a symptom of a mental state that is causing overeating rather than a cause of it. TV viewing also tends to be an urban activity and, as Sonia Livingstone and her colleagues have demonstrated,[27] excessive viewing by children is an aspect of a screen-based lifestyle that has developed because of the perceived lack of safety in urban public spaces. In the UK, many parents actively encourage their children to stay at home to watch TV (or to use new-screen entertainments) because they are reluctant to allow them to roam in the traffic-dominated environment of the modern city. This further reduces their opportunities for outdoor exercise which have already been reduced or excluded entirely from school provision. The perceived hostility of the urban environment is also a cause of adults avoiding venturing out, and television content is often conveniently saddled with the blame for encouraging this perception. Such causal links often allege that TV is 'saturated' with images of urban violence, and that it 'bombards' its viewers with them. Both these emotive terms are at odds with a contemporary TV whose output is mainly concerned with domestic issues.

The health lobby has identified a link between large amounts of TV viewing and large amounts of body fat. Whether the link is causal or coincidental is important. Blaming TV as the main cause means less attention is paid to other more persuasive factors, from the perceived hostility of the urban environment to the poor quality of cheap foods dominated by sugar and fat. It is remarkable that while some medical research attempts to link TV to a lack of activity, the TV and marketing industries are becoming alarmed by an opposing trend in the lack of attention paid to TV by multi-taskers, and in particular their distressing tendency to ignore or bypass commercials.**»** It seems that there are as many couch subverters as there are couch potatoes, and many of them seem to be younger members of the TV audience.

» Q42

Q11 Does TV make you fat?

Is there too much violence on TV?

Discussions about violence and TV have a depressing sameness about them. Especially in the UK, 'violence' and 'sex' are often linked together as two phenomena that cause much indignation in moralistic approaches to TV content. Along with this comes a concern about the effects of TV portrayals of violence on people in general and vulnerable people in particular. It is alleged that seeing violence on TV makes people more aggressive, or at least more accepting of violence around them. Much research has been undertaken to establish whether this is the case. However, laboratory experiments that, for example, expose groups of children to violent images to measure their attitudes before and after all suffer from the same problem. They try, as far as possible, to eliminate extraneous social factors in order to concentrate on a single set of causal relationships between what is seen and the immediately subsequent behaviour of those children. The concentration is therefore on short-term effects, but often long-term consequences are deduced from them. The elimination of wider social factors also predetermines the outcome of such experiments, as it is just as likely that wider social factors lie behind the wide range of responses that are exhibited to the same example of 'violence' by differing people. Any attempt to demonstrate a link between TV images and particular kinds of behaviour

» Q11

suffers from the same problem.** Yet violence remains a real issue in society and for television, and a number of questions should be answered about it.

The first is what 'violence' actually means. It is a category that brings together a number of different kinds of action. Verbal violence can produce as intense a response in viewers as physical violence, especially as it contains both menace and humiliation. Physical violence as a category includes both attacks by one person on another and the physical destruction of property like buildings and cars. The kind of mayhem produced by car chases, explosions and other such activity has a very different emotional effect from interpersonal violence. There is no fear or sense of threat attached to such actions. Instead, the emotions they evoke are more child-like and even celebratory, as these rituals of destruction relate to a what-if sense of crossing the boundary between the everyday logic of things and its subversion, a sheer delight in disorder. In such mayhem, the human beings who are involved are reduced to figures in a landscape. Their injuries are not shown, and there is no potential for empathy with them. At some level, they are figures who are rather inconveniently in the way of the real business of the destruction of the physical order of things. Such violence is governed by clear generic rules, and to show real injury, apart from a few decorative scratches on the protagonists, would be to break one of the cardinal rules of the genre and destroy the particular kind of anarchic thrill provoked by the events. This contrasts strongly with other categories of violence. Attacks by one person on another within TV fiction involve known characters. The level of violence will be less, but the emotions evoked will be more complicated, and closely bound up in what we feel for those characters and their plight. They will include fear, exhilaration and distaste in varied proportions.

On TV, such actions take place within defined narrative and generic forms. Violence in news bulletins is different from violence in cartoons; physical mayhem and destruction differ from attacks on or by characters established by the drama; an attack on a character in a suspense or horror film is different from an attack on a character in a soap opera. The same gestures will have different meanings in each context, and there are different levels of acceptable portrayal in each context. Yet all of these are 'violence on TV'. In each case, the 'violence' has different consequences. In a cartoon the actions are excessive but have few if any consequences. In a soap, a relatively restrained act of violence like a slap to the face can have devastating consequences for familial relations for a long time. Violence in news bulletins is more a matter of consequences than action. News rarely features footage of actual acts of violence, unless safely from a great

Q12 Is there too much violence on TV?

distance. But it commonly shows the devastating aftermath of institutional violence in footage from armed conflicts around the globe. Early evening bulletins tend to sanitise this footage to take account of the legitimate criticism that

» Q43 many children who watch will be disturbed by it.**»**

The question is further complicated by asking who is watching and in what state of mind. Any TV depiction will encounter people in different states of mind and at different stages in their lives. The problem of any general regulation of these various kinds of depiction of 'violence' is the fact that television is a universal medium, addressed to all and sundry. The vast majority of viewers are capable of distinguishing between fiction and fact, of understanding generic codes, and of understanding a narrative that shows the consequences of violence in a condemnatory way. For almost everyone, these understandings permeate their enjoyment of fiction and their appreciation of factual material. We know it to be a depiction rather than a transcription of reality. Indeed, this is why we want to watch in the first place, to be told a story organised

» Q15 towards some kind of conclusion.**»**

However, the mental state of a tiny number of people prevents them from participating in such understandings. Regulation does not address such rare and extreme cases, except in those tragic criminal cases where TV (or film) is used as a convenient causal explanation for a psychotic act. Then there is a brief outcry for tighter censorship which can sometimes even result in legislation. Instead, regulation, both self-regulation and the rules governing broadcasting, determines the general level of portrayal in sensitive areas like that of violence. These set the level of expectancy in a particular cultural context, so that TV violence in one

» Q26 country will seem very different to a foreign viewer.**»** In the UK, standards are set by regulators in relation to the most vulnerable in the community, principally children. Different levels of violence are permitted before and after the 9pm watershed, and the practices around news footage initiated by the BBC produce a further level of inhibition regarding what can be shown, even in bulletins

» Q43 after 9pm.**»**

Some research has concentrated on the effects of depictions of violence not on behaviour so much as on perceptions of the outside world. If TV mediates the wider world to the domestic space of ordinary life, then it follows that the depiction of a world permeated by acts of violence will lead to a perception that this is what the world is like. Such a perception can exaggerate the risks of stepping outside the front door; or alternatively can encourage an understanding of the nature of the global community» and a degree of empathy with distant others.» The result in either case is the possibility of discussion of the issue and the will to construct less violent means for the resolution of disputes in society. This long process would be helped by a greater discrimination between types of depiction of violence rather than the use of a single homogenising category.

Q9
Q16

Q12 Is there too much violence on TV?

What's the point of Jade Goody?

Jade Goody sprang to public attention in the third UK series of *Big Brother* in 2002 with her spectacular displays of boorishness and ignorance. She became a lightning rod for public anxiety about education standards, since her ignorance of global issues was profound ('America? Do they speak English there?'), and was a useful point of comparison for both behaviour and looks ('at least I'm better looking than Jade' or 'at least I'm not a loudmouth like her'). After *Big Brother*, she remained in the public eye, cheerfully revealing the ups and downs of her life to any publication that would give her space, and being followed by cable channel Living TV for the opening of a beauty salon in the autumn of 2005.

In 2007, she appeared in *Celebrity Big Brother* along with film director Ken Russell, singers Jermaine Jackson and Leo Sayer, and Bollywood star Shilpa Shetty. Her attack on Shetty in a dispute about how to cook chicken led to accusations of racism, 40,000 complaints to the regulatory body Ofcom and the withdrawal of the programme's sponsorship by Carphone Warehouse. Jade's brand of perfume (Shhh...) was also withdrawn from the shelves of many stores. Acres of newspaper publicity were generated and *Big Brother*'s flagging ratings revived. But Jade had gone too far, both in her racism and in her bullying (despite being patron of an anti-bullying charity). Her tearful contrition in newspaper interviews focused a public debate on the persistent level of racism in British society, but it damaged her career as a celebrity. Jade had reached the limits of celebrity by the sheer venom of her attack on Shetty, who went on to win and to voice her forgiveness of Jade. Jade had found that her public role as a celebrity was not, after all, a licence to say whatever she felt like saying. Celebrity, for those who attain it, is a self-nourishing phenomenon, and can even be contagious. But it also requires that celebrities continue to be useful as public points of reference. Jade Goody performed the role of the ultimate celebrity: known for what she did not know. She had performed this role with a certain style that some even called 'loveable'.[28] Her over-aggressive assertion of racist views proved her undoing because she stepped out of that role.

TV is certainly not the only source of celebrities, but all celebrities will pass through TV at a crucial point in their professional development. Television celebrity is the moment when someone known for something becomes someone known for being known. Celebrities are created from media attention, so can come from any area of activity that gains the attention of any medium. Celebrities are created by sport, movies, the music business and by the specialist press, by society gossip columns and even by political activity. There comes a point when celebrities need to leap from the local notoriety of their chosen line of activity, and become, in that wonderful phrase of the last century, 'a household name'. This is where television is crucial: it provides celebrities with the forum to make the leap into the general and non-specific.**》** A man named Fran Cosgrove was a security guard for the group Westlife; he briefly dated a member of the girl band Atomic Kitten and so entered the specialist teen music press and its spin-off newspaper columns. It was a last-minute booking on the ITV series *I'm a Celebrity Get Me Out of Here!* in 2004 that brought him to a wide enough public to merit being singled out as a celebrity. From there it was a short step to the ill-fated ITV format failure *Celebrity Love Island* in 2005. Rebecca Loos gained her momentary notoriety for her kiss-and-tell revelations about her affair with the then England football captain David Beckham. The reality formats *The Farm* on Five and *Celebrity Love Island* (where she appeared with Cosgrove) defined her as a celebrity.

Celebrity is contagious, and television is the place where it is most easily caught. But when a celebrity graduates to TV, that celebrity is transformed into someone who is expected to take a public role, to be able to act as the presenter of a programme, to have views on current issues, to create a book or to provide a regular supply of stories for the press. This is not itself a new development, as the views of public figures on mundane and important issues

Q13 What's the point of Jade Goody?

have been sought by the popular press since it developed in the late nineteenth century. But the increased social emphasis on emotional issues in the post-war era of TV has put fresh demands on society's stock of celebrities. They are now required to be a convenient source of stories about health and emotional problems as well as views on issues of the day. The growth in magazine titles along with the increasing number of pages in newspapers since the 1960s has also increased the demand for celebrity information. Sometimes there is substantial income to be earned from this, through exclusives, advances on ghosted autobiographies and product endorsement. So celebrity has now become a way of earning a living, but it is not as easy as it seems. Jade Goody is the only contestant from *Big Brother* after six years to have become an enduring public figure, and she has done so only because she has a startling lack of sensitivity about the comments made about her.

Television bestows on celebrities the magic of being generally known, but the price is that they should nevertheless be known for their emotional difficulties. The purpose of celebrities is at once mythic and mundane. They provide a focus for the discussion of issues like health, lifestyle choices, relationships, relatives: important issues for everyone but 'mundane' ones that do not regularly feature in the domain of political debate. Celebrities focus these issues by revealing their cancer hell or their tense relations with their siblings, mainly in the pages of newspapers and magazines, but also on the couches of daytime TV. Celebrity gossip provides a common space for the exchange of information and views about common problems and anxieties. Celebrities have an important role, but it is a restricted one, existing at a level below stardom. Several female celebrities have revealed that they are being treated for breast cancer, but it took a star like Kylie Minogue to bring the issue to wide attention, triggering a leap in the numbers seeking breast examinations. Celebrities are not stars. Those who retain their status are as likely to be famous for being ordinary as they are famous for being famous.

To survive, celebrities need to develop an instinctive understanding of their mundane mythic role. For there are many temporary celebrities who do not understand this mythic role, and they tend to be those whose celebrity is the direct product of TV itself. The participants in *Big Brother* are engaged in an activity of defining the boundaries of acceptable inter-personal behaviour.**»** This is the public role of such a programme, and it is distinct from their own motives for appearing on the show, and indeed from the incentives, real or implied, that are offered by the production company.**»** This is a mythic role; these individuals are a more civilised version of human sacrifice or public executions, offered as an example for the rest of us to meditate on.

The principal reason why the mythic process of celebrity is more civilised lies in its temporary nature. Television creates temporary celebrities because of the event status and now-ness of TV.**»** At the end of the event, they can return to their previous lives chastened or made wiser. The nature of their celebrity is that they will be soon forgotten, that people will remember them vaguely for having been a participant rather than for the persona that they tried to adopt during that series. They will carry the aura of 'having been on TV' rather than, as many still assume, being stuck with the extreme and possibly objectionable characteristics they seemed to display at the time. There are distinct advantages to being famous for just fifteen minutes, in Andy Warhol's prescient phrase. Temporary celebrity allows its participants to see that fame has many drawbacks, including public disapproval, typecasting and the enforced company of other celebrities and their egos.

However, the market in celebrities tends to intervene here. The participants in temporary but important mythic events like *Big Brother* or *The X Factor* can be easily misled into believing that they have something durable and extraordinary to offer to society in general. They are seduced into proposing themselves as enduring celebrities. There is nothing sadder than the former reality TV participant washed up on the shores of celebrity-for-celebrity's sake. The subsequent difficulties of their

Q13 What's the point of Jade Goody?

everyday lives are chronicled in specialised publications like *Heat*, which, fascinating though they are, consist largely of gossip about gossip and body shape. The companies that produce reality TV sometimes encourage this delusion by acting as agents for the participants because they are eager to milk every possible income stream. Eking out temporary celebrity denies the essence of reality TV celebrity. Reality TV celebrity is confined to the moment of the mythic performance that the individual undertakes for the amusement and edification of the wider public. Only a few manage to find the resources to play an enduring role as a celebrity, continuing to play a role as the convenient material for mundane myths and contemporary debate.

Who was that?

There is a plentiful supply of celebrities as a result of the expansion of TV. A London radio show[29] regularly featured a challenge to listeners to 'bag a celebrity' on the street and make them phone the radio station for a live conversation. A donation to the celebrity's charity would result; but not for every celebrity, only for the best celebrity of the day. Celebrity recognition on the streets of London is a common enough event for such a regular feature to be feasible. It is a result of the intimacy of our relationship with television performers.

It is a common enough experience for the inhabitants of major cities to see someone on the street whom they vaguely recognise. Not infrequently, it turns out to be no actual acquaintance at all, but someone who has been seen on TV. It may be a minor actor, a reporter or newsreader, or simply someone who has appeared in a factual programme. One night, I watched a BBC Three programme called *Dog Borstal*, which took an hour to demonstrate the retraining of owners who had lost control of their dogs. A week later, I saw one of these owners, still struggling with his outsized dog as they came down a street near my home. In this case, I could place this distinctive man-and-dog combo instantly. The week-long retraining that had been the programme's subject had clearly been of limited use. Seasoned TV performers report a rather different phenomenon. People come up to them, convinced that they really do know each other. When the TV face denies it, the individual may realise their mistake and recognise them, but not infrequently they need to be told 'you must recognise me from TV' before they realise what is going on.

This vividly demonstrates one of the more curious aspects of the televisual experience. Faces become familiar in the same way that the faces of everyday individuals become familiar. The recognition that we accord to TV faces is the same recognition as that which we give to people we have met once or twice at parties, down the pub, or fleetingly at work. It is an instant reaction, one which acknowledges the need to greet that person. In the ordinary crowded street of a city, it is normal to scan hundreds of faces swiftly without greeting or in any way acknowledging that a meeting has taken place. This is the essence of the urban experience where the norm is to encounter strangers with minimal interaction. However, to pass an acquaintance in the street is still taken as a breach of normal polite human interaction. The reaction is 'you blanked me' or 'you ignored me', to which the accepted reply is 'I was in another world' or possibly 'I didn't recognise you behind those dark glasses'. A lack of recognition is resented and has to be explained because the natural expectation is that we should be spontaneously recognised by our acquaintances.

So it is often the case that TV faces are greeted as acquaintances before the person greeting has worked out what the nature of the acquaintanceship might be. The need to greet is an urgent one, and an entirely natural one. The curious aspect is not that TV faces are greeted, but the difficulty that many have in placing their recognition as being TV-based rather than real-life-based. The intimacy of the TV relationship might be a sufficient reason, were it not for one more complicating factor. The recognition is extended to actors, not in their fictional roles but simply as known faces just like any other acquaintance. The actor might have been seen in all kinds of dramatic situations, but the recognition does not extend to a spontaneous association of murder, mayhem, tragedy or farce with that face. It is simply a generalised recognition. The soap actor is the exception here. Most people will make an association of the flesh-and-blood actor in front of them and the fictional role played by that actor only in the case of actors who have a long-running role. In that case, they may well be greeted with their fictional name, indicating that the recogniser has a clear sense of the basis of their recognition.

Other than this rare case of actors 'trapped' in a role, the act of spontaneous recognition of a TV face is also one of misrecognition. The face is classed as an acquaintance:

someone whom we know but do not know well. A link or engagement of some kind is felt, but this is not correct, at least in the sense that it is not a reciprocal feeling. The recognition is not mutual, and the TV face can feel no tie or social obligation towards the person recognising them. However, the recogniser does feel that there is some connection implying a mutual social tie. This can easily be negotiated when misrecognising an actor as an acquaintance, but it becomes more significant when the sphere of TV meets other spheres. The phenomenon of recognition/misrecognition of TV faces has a major impact on public affairs and politics.**»** This intimate recognition/ misrecognition is a distinct and new kind of experience, and is an important effect of TV as a domestic and everyday medium.

‣ Q7

Q14 Who was that?

II Questions about TV genres

Q15 Does the news make us anxious?

News creates anxiety because it tells stories with no known ending. Most stories have an end in view, an end to which they are working. But, by definition, the news story cannot be working towards an end. News is an update on the unfolding stories of the real world. Having no predictable ending or even predicted development, news stories are very different from fiction, where planning some distance ahead is built into the working of the form, even in a series like *Lost*, where the eventual ending may be hazy even to the producers and scriptwriters.**»** TV series fiction at least provides the satisfactions of incidents that resolve, narratives that begin and end within one episode, and an overall series structure of a given number of episodes each season. News has none of that. The only certainty is that there will always be news, and little of it will be good.

News stories provoke anxiety by providing ongoing updates that evoke many of the strong emotions associated with fictional narratives, but have no ability to provide a satisfying ending... or any ending at all. TV news coverage has grown in extent, depth and regularity since the early 1980s. Longer news bulletins, the growth of new channels including twenty-four-hour rolling news, together with technologies allowing instant reporting, have transformed TV news into an ongoing update rather than a report on something that has already happened. This narrative uncertainty creates anxiety. An indication of how widespread this anxiety is can be found in the increasing use of rolling news services after 9/11, during the Iraq War of 2003[30] or the suicide bombings on the London Underground of July 2005. Most of the millions watching soon find that they have no direct involvement. Thankfully, their immediate family and friends will not have been affected. Yet they continue to be involved as witnesses to the unfolding of a drama with no controlling scriptwriters, a drama that involved people like themselves.**»** Any drama involves moments of anxiety, which is the reason why people seek out programmes that involve suspense, scenes in which the characters are in jeopardy, or sequences of explicit violence. But the level is increased – perhaps beyond the strictly pleasurable – when people find themselves caught up as spectators to a story whose ending is unknown.

In response to this anxiety, news has sought not only to tell what has happened, but to predict what might happen next. In an effort to deal with this, as well as to appear as 'up-to-the-minute' as possible, news bulletins have increasingly taken to including material that seeks to anticipate the future. In its simplest form, this can be seen in those items that begin 'The government is expected today to...' (based on press releases) or 'New regulations coming into force today will force X to Y' (leading to interviews with those affected, who tell how their livelihoods/homes/loved ones might be impinged upon). As this habit of predictive news has developed, it has forced the development of a rhetoric of trust in TV news bulletins. Different roles are trusted to speak different truths and are assumed to require different kinds of trust.

Those news broadcasters that continue to claim a level of objectivity build levels of trust into their bulletins. It is not the role of the news anchors or studio presenters themselves to speculate; their role is factual, and their presentation is confined to matters of fact as they have been discovered by the news-gathering operation. It is not the news presenters' role to get upset about stories, nor to push an explicit line in the language they use. The presenters or anchors embody the news provider, and so need to be perceived as objective rather than partisan. They provide a privileged view for the TV audience, bringing together information from disparate points of view into a **》** Q16 coherent narrative.**》** As a result, they have to talk to other people whose position allows them to speculate about the future. Now, in the era of the live link, the anchor is able to converse with two distinct categories of journalists, both of whom are able to provide different kinds of speculation about the future.

In specific locations there are reporters whose views are circumscribed by their location. If they are reporting on a court case, their speculation might well be enough to satisfy the question 'what will happen next?' In more complex stories that are developing on a number of fronts (a diplomatic stand-off, a war etc) the on-the-spot reporter's ability to generalise is limited. At this point, all they can share is the rumours they have heard and the speculations current in their immediate vicinity. Reporters are trusted to tell the truth as they find it, where they find it, but limited by the extent of their view. They bear witness to what they have seen, and, like all who bear witness, they are expected to be as truthful as possible.[31] This is particularly marked in the case of modern war reporting, when 'embeds', the reporters travelling with troops, are usually very careful to emphasise the partiality of their view.

The reporter's level is the 'here and now'. A second level of journalist has the job of providing the 'there and then'. This is the correspondent who, in studio or on location, brings together these situated truths and speculations. The correspondent sees the larger picture and provides more definitive 'analysis', which more often than not is the term used for speculation about the future. The correspondent's role is explicitly to provide such material, switching easily from a summary of the factors and personalities involved to an outline of the next events in the unfolding story. Some correspondents will offer more than one prediction, outlining what will happen if the vote goes well or goes badly for the Prime Minister, and what might happen in the event of a defeat. In this way, narrative anxiety is reduced as there is seen to be a pattern to the events ahead, a set of narrative possibilities fanning out from the moment in which we stand into the future that remains uncertain. The act of providing an exhaustive list of probable outcomes reduces this uncertainty to more manageable levels. Viewers are no longer faced with the awesome possibility that anything might happen, but just with the expectation that life will continue along defined routes.

News has used the live link to develop a rhetorical structure of truthfulness that can accommodate speculation about the future and so reduce anxiety. It can be difficult to reconcile this predictive function with the trust that is invested in news organisations that they will tell the truth, or at least try to do so. As no one can tell what will happen next, the speculations can scarcely be said to be truthful in the same way as reports of the present and recent past. But they are needed nonetheless. A news bulletin does not consist of just one story. It contains many varied events that have taken place in the previous twenty-four hours. The news bulletin reminds its audience, sometimes too forcibly, of the complexity and simultaneity of daily events. There is so much happening in the world all at the same time. There are so many disparate and desperate situations, none of them with a resolution in sight. In this complicated and uncertain world, the news bulletin's speculative predictions of the future are valuable in reducing anxiety and uncertainty to some kind of pattern, however provisional it is, and however wrong it turns out to be.

Does too much horror stop people caring?

Watching terrible events is both fascinating and intolerable. Something forces you to go on watching, often the desire for some kind of explanation and order. Some events simply become unwatchably horrible because of the sheer scale of their outrage against basic human values. The Beslan school siege of 2004 was one such event, where a whole school in the Russian republic of North Ossetia was taken hostage on the first day of term. From the outset, the siege became a media event. The suffering of the children, denied food and water for three days, was accompanied by a general incompetence among the Russian troops surrounding the school, and the cause that motivated the hostage-takers remains unclear. After three days, the outcome was absolutely shocking: the killing of over 350 people, over half of them young children. The events seemed to have no explanation other than a desire to kill as many Russians as possible, and particularly the children.

There was a widespread reaction of not wanting to watch the footage of Beslan as it was broadcast. As one seasoned TV reviewer wrote:

> [I found] the point where I couldn't go on watching TV even though every fibre of my being was telling me I should, the Friday before last, at the top of the news, as a man carried the limp and bloodied body of a dead child from the smouldering shell of the Beslan school, at which point I got up and walked out of the room. After a couple of decades spent sating an unquenchable thirst for news, for the first time I had hit a wall. Last Tuesday [I saw] perhaps the most horrific piece of footage I have ever seen: the Beslan hostage-takers' video from inside the school, which I viewed through my fingers, head-in-hands, shaking in disbelief.[32]

This reviewer, Katherine Flett, was not alone. These were images shot by the hostage-takers, but for what purpose? Possibly they wanted to use them to demonstrate their bargaining position; possibly to document their exploit. In any case, being shown these images crossed a boundary for many people. Some found it intolerable to see the misery of those about to die. Others felt they were seeing the siege from the inside, and were not enlightened. It left them even further away from comprehending why these events should be happening at all, why humans should do this to each other.**

» Q12

Flett comes close to accusing TV of showing things that no one has a right to see, and is similar to that of Tom Junod's observation about watching the Twin Towers of New York's World Trade Center burning on 11 September 2001:

> Dozens, scores, maybe hundreds of people died by leaping from a burning building, and we have somehow taken it upon ourselves to deem their deaths unworthy of witness – because we have somehow deemed the act of witness, in this one regard, unworthy of us.[33]

Complex emotions are stirred up by having what, in the end, is a privileged view: Junod points to a sense of guilt, Flett to a feeling of revulsion not only at the horrific act itself, but equally at the fact of being able to see it. Both the Beslan siege and the Twin Towers were live events, unfolding as viewers watched, and so intensified the emotions of those who watched them on TV. A significant part of the horror and the involvement came from seeing the actual catastrophe unfold as it happened, but being powerless to do anything about them. This was an extreme version of one of the basic effects of TV: bringing different spaces together in the same moment in time. It gives a simultaneous feeling of connection and powerlessness which is very disturbing. It compels the viewer to try both to share and to understand the events, but also makes them uncomfortably aware of the privileged position of witnessing that they occupy. These emotions are present in any activity of watching, but the liveness of these events» and their unexpectedness highlighted and intensified these feelings. Both the Beslan siege and the attack on the World Trade Center show how the TV witnessing of terrible events is characterised by a struggle to comprehend first what was happening and then why it was happening. The images themselves were not enough, however often they were repeated as they were in the case of the Twin Towers. Viewers of such live events cannot 'just see' them, treating them as just another spectacle from which they are distant. All the many viewers of such live events are called to witness them: to occupy not the same physical space but the same space of awareness as these events which are taking place at the same moment but in another place. The events then require explanation. We the viewers need to know what it is that we have seen so that we can integrate it with our understanding of our world.»

This is where TV coverage becomes a complex seeing, very different from observations of an eyewitness or participant. Multiple viewpoints come together to create explanations and, in so doing, the viewer is put in a privileged position in relation to the events. We see more than participants; we see through many points of view, and we are offered a range of explanations. The process of explanation has three stages. First is the examination, through interviews with participants and onlookers, of emotions, motives and psychological states that were involved. Then comes the conjuring of pattern from the onrush of witnessing, the creation of an overall narrative account of what actually happened. Finally there comes a wider activity of fitting these events into what is already known about the world: not so much into the context of the events themselves, but more into general understandings of how the world is. This process I have called 'working through'.[34]

Few cataclysmic events are covered live, so the initial need to understand what we are seeing is already taken care of by forms of narration and contextualisation. TV is rarely there on the scene of a tragedy as it happens, but

Q16 Does too much horror stop people caring?

it is increasingly there immediately afterwards. A disaster strikes, and we initially view the aftermath. Actual footage of the sudden and unexpected will emerge a little later. Live news coverage of rescue attempts is then supplemented by material produced by those sucked up into the events on various digital imaging devices. This was the case with both the Indian Ocean Tsunami of December 2004 and the London bombings of July 2005. Very quickly news organisations picked up video footage of the arrival of the tsunami shot from hotel balconies and mobile phone footage from inside the Underground tunnels in London. This 'citizen-journalist' footage was inserted into a larger account that included other points of view, of reporters and eyewitnesses, victims and rescuers. In the case of such events, which continue to unfold as they are reported, any simple live witness is already pulled into the immediate rush to find the story, to put some kind of narrative structure or generalising view onto the events, to assess their scale and impact. Any terrible event, especially one that involves live or vivid images, is immediately the trigger for a process of trying to understand, to get accounts of some kind. With 9/11, relatively incoherent accounts over the phone were put on air in order to get the multiplicity of points of view. An account is assembled as soon as possible:

> In the live coverage of breaking news, as time moves on implacably, the newsroom is journeying forwards into the unknown, while looking back over its shoulder in a continuing effort to catch up with and make sense of what has just now happened. Continuously aware that, from moment to moment, new viewers are joining the programme, the presenters regularly re-cap and summarize what has thus far happened and what is thus far known about what has happened. Along the way incoming bits of information are added to the snowballing narrative.[35]

Most events come to air after several pieces of information have already been brought together. So they come to air pre-processed, already understood in their bare outline, and organised into some kind of provisional account.**»** What follows immediately is a push to individualise. Terrible events are too large to comprehend easily, so personal scale aids comprehension. When something big and incomprehensible begins to take place, there is an immediate televisual reaction to try to measure its impact on individual psychologies. The people involved are strangers, unknown to us, yet somehow we seek to know who they are. In mass horrors, there is a search for individual stories, and then for individual motives. With the 9/11 attack, early commentary tried to attribute motives to the falling bodies seen emerging from the top floors of the buildings, and this process of individualising was pushed further than is usually the case because of the traumatic nature of the attack for US culture. Initially, they were seen as people choosing to jump to their deaths rather than to await another form of dying:

> To be sure, some who fell didn't jump. Witnesses say a few people seemed to have stumbled out of broken windows obscured by smoke. But most say those jumping appeared to make a conscious choice to die by falling rather than from smoke, heat or fire. Ultimately, they were choosing not whether to die but how to die. Nobody survived on the floors from which people jumped.[36]

As Tom Junod put it, 'To be sure, no one will ever know… but we still need to speculate.'[37] And Junod continued to speculate, trying to piece together the case of one particular individual whose dramatic picture appeared on many newspaper front pages in the immediate aftermath. Junod sought out his identity and story. His reportage itself became the subject of a documentary, thinking further about the falling man, his identity and his possible motive. The process becomes one of forensic examination of the available evidential footage.**»** Henry Singer's 2006 documentary *The Falling Man*[38] pushes this process of speculation about the man's identity about as far as it

Q16 Does too much horror stop people caring?

81

will go, and possibly beyond the point of usefulness. For this speculation will end only at the point where it began: the impossibility of knowing what any individual in these circumstances chose (or was forced) to do.

Usually, the search for emotions and motives is satisfied by eyewitness statements, by the snatched interviews with dazed individuals as they stumble away from the crisis. They are often unaware of the scale of the event in which they are caught up, a scale which we are witnessing from our privileged view. These eyewitnesses bring us back to the realisation of the partial view that individuals inevitably have of events. They express their gratitude ·to rescuers, their luck at having survived at all, their concerns for missing companions or worrying relatives. Yet their language usually falls short of the experience we are witnessing. They lived a fragment of it; we see its totality. That is possibly the first thing we comprehend about the difference between their situation and ours as privileged viewers. We see more, but experience less. The personal stories therefore have a double function. First they enable us as viewers to relate to the events, to empathise with those individuals. Then they enable us to understand our relation to those events, our place as distanced observers.

The second stage of the coverage takes the bare sequence of events, the vivid contributions of participants and the 'best' images collated from many sources. It combines them into a coherent narrative, which anticipates future events.**》** As Paddy Scannell shows in his analysis of the coverage of 9/11: 'At first it was utterly incomprehensible but, by the end of the day, the situation had been accurately analysed and correctly understood. Immediate action had been taken and future courses of action predicted and assessed.'[39] This is what distinguishes a narrative from an account, which is a mere sequence of events. There are causes and there are consequences. The terrible event has meanings that can be picked over. It was itself the result of other events and the actions of known individuals or of natural forces that news will often dramatise through animated graphics. It will lead to actions that, in the (often vain) words of politicians, can 'ensure that this can never

》 Q15

happen again'. We know the scale of suffering and have seen some of the individuals who have suffered; we may even know what they intend to do now and who will help them. We have heard the experts and the correspondents who are able to draw out the underlying meanings. This process of narrativising is seen by some critics as one of distortion.» However, to accuse TV of 'distortion' is to miss what is going on here. It is the formation of the event as a public and shared event, one that is known collectively and can be referred to by a shorthand term: 'the tsunami', 'the London bombings', '9/11', 'Srebrenica', 'Darfur'. The news process makes the event into a universal cultural phenomenon.»

The process has a third stage which takes place some way from the original coverage. This is the more difficult process of trying to comprehend the relation between these terrible events and the everyday. They may be rare, and we can but wish that they should be rarer still. Some are exceptional natural events, as a hurricane or earthquake is exceptional. But many involve human agency from their conception to their grisly conclusion. They involve people doing ordinary things but for destructive motives. They involve people who, given another time or place, might well have been ourselves. Such events change our common perceptions of everyday life, precisely because we have been swept up into the process of witnessing TV news events. More explanations follow. We have analysis programmes and documentaries like *The Falling Man*. Fiction moves in to render aspects of the events in forms that are both more graphic and more psychologised. Fiction series like *Spooks* deal week after week with terrorist threats. The terrible event slowly becomes something with which we live, and something with which we have come to terms. In the end, this is a process of caring, one of discovering the interconnectedness of humanity. It is equally one of demonising, of defining particular kinds of strangers as beyond that community of humanity. Categories like paedophile or terrorist lie outside the realm of comprehension and empathy that is created by this process of coming to terms with terrible events.

Q16 Does too much horror stop people caring?

Where the events take place in a distant and unfamiliar political and social context, to witness them at a distance risks bringing on a general lassitude. This is a pressing knowledge that horrors have happened far away, and that there is nothing that viewing individuals can do about them. At this point, the stories of survivors, or case studies of known victims, serve a very particular purpose. They anchor the general, distant event in the specific and the intimate. They bring the density of human experience to the generality of a far-flung place. They appeal to a common humanity, or more precisely to a common understanding of humanity. If these strangers too had their lives and hopes, if they were going about their everyday business until swept up into these incomprehensible events, then a feeling of empathy with them makes the events that bit more comprehensible. As distanced observers, we know ourselves to be nevertheless part of the same

» 09

world.» Nevertheless, television is better at covering some catastrophes than others. Contrary to the view held by many, it is not geographic distance that determines the amount and effectiveness of TV coverage. Many claim that a distant tragedy that does not involve Europeans or Americans will receive less coverage, along the lines of Claude Cockburn's candidate for the most boring *Times* headline 'Small Earthquake in Chile: Not Many Dead'.[40] Such attitudes are less and less true now that satellite news coverage is increasingly global in its reach. TV will give major coverage to such sudden disasters whenever there is available footage. However, there is less coverage of longer term catastrophes like famines which develop more slowly.

The sheer volume of news stories, especially tragic ones, leads to the view that TV audiences are somehow 'compassion fatigued'. Though a fashionable view amongst the cynical, this perception probably does not accord with the reactions of most TV viewers. Even the idea of 'compassion fatigue' was not coined in relation to TV – it was invented by charities to explain falling donations. This fall in income could equally be ascribed to increased competition between charities and the often aggressive attempts that they have used to raise money, including telethons.[41] Compassion fatigue is not the result of TV coverage of terrible events, mainly because television's own seeing and showing is more complex, and involves a realisation of how distant we are from those events along with a realisation of what responses might be appropriate from that distance. TV rarely witnesses terrible events as they happen, and even then it immediately begins to show them from many points of view rather than the position of a single observer. This distanced and privileged view is distinctive, and is a product of television. It produces a general awareness of some of the crucial problems of our shared world.

Q17

Why do TV stories never seem to come to an end?

Television is full of stories. Storytelling is one of the oldest and most enjoyable ways of examining and arriving at an understanding of people and the world. The span of a story explores the complexity of events and peoples' actions and reactions, and promises an ending that will usually provide an overall moral perspective. Yet endings are relatively rare on television. More often they are provisional, so that the regular characters can return, or explicitly delayed, with factual series promising that in the next episode we will see the outcome of this week's events. And we know that next week fresh dilemmas will emerge whose resolution will again be delayed. Finality, definitive closure, is rare in television.

» Q22

Why should this be? Surely it would be better if television provided complete and satisfying stories? Indeed, this was a strong belief among TV professionals early in the medium's history.» Nowadays, television is for ever in the middle of things. This is in part because the real pleasure of being told a story lies in the events in the middle, after the introduction of the character and the basic dilemmas or enigmas, and before the whole thing is satisfyingly wrapped up. We enjoy the ways that characters are frustrated from achieving their goals and have to use all their resources to get where they want, or gain, through experience, the wisdom that allows them to see the pointlessness of their initial aims.

Television prolongs this process by multiplying incidents. More things happen to regular TV characters than happen to their viewers. This can lead to a certain aura of unreality about the events, especially around the more unfortunate soap-opera characters (and when was there ever a fortunate soap character who was not 'riding for a fall', expecting an imminent dose of hubris?). Too many disasters befall soap characters, especially those in the more extravagant series. They are at the extreme end of a general tendency in TV storytelling. This tendency provides its viewers with frequent resolution of narrative incidents rather than the definitive closure of a narrative with all the loose ends tied up and the characters dispatched to death or a serene future. It's 'off they go back to all their other worries' rather than 'they all live happily ever after'. The types of incidents which are contained and resolved within the larger narrative include the resolution of a police investigation or a law case, the reconciliation of arguing neighbours or the agreement of reluctant parents to a marriage. They provide a sense of narrative closure. The enduring characters in the series may well have learned from them and been changed by them. And they offer the seeds of further narrative incidents: a fresh row between neighbours or the subsequent divorce of the happy couple. It seems that these incidents are enough to satisfy the demand for satisfactory stories, and that definitive endings are not essential.

This certainly fits with some forms of storytelling, which is why television has been defined as a 'bardic' form.[42] There is even a school of thought that argues that some forms of drama are more enjoyable because their endings are less than satisfactory. Feminist critics of melodrama[43] have claimed that the relatively perfunctory endings to many Hollywood film melodramas of the 1950s are 'tacked on' because the dilemmas they portrayed could have no satisfactory resolution in the society of that time. Films like *All that Heaven Allows* provided a powerful expression of the frustrated desire of women, hemmed in by social convention. And, as the title implies, heaven does not really allow very much to those who want to follow their desires. In such films, the emotions stirred up, the sense of identification with the characters and the obviousness of the proper (but socially forbidden or even immoral) ending all overwhelm the official ending. The films are seen by such critics as 'better' to the extent that their final closure does not work.

With television, the delay in closure means that characters can learn from their mistakes. What television seems to offer through this process is a very modern and secular form of salvation. Characters are saved in this world and not the next, and see their rewards in this world. Those who redeem themselves are saved by learning, through experience and understanding their experience. Those who do not learn from experience are quite possibly sitcom characters, who the format dictates will never learn.**»** Or they are simply ejected from the narrative, sent to far-flung destinations or off to join the pile of forgotten corpses that most TV dramas create for themselves. Learning, and with it salvation, takes the form of the transformation of character. Bad-tempered asocial characters begin to show signs of consideration and generosity. Aggressive characters rein in their tempers often with visible effort. There will be backsliding and major relapses as with any reformed sinners, but they will be treated as reformed characters increasingly as the series evolves. This transformation through socialisation is a major theme of factual programming and reality TV as much as it is of series fiction.**»**

» Q18

» Q25

From the audience point of view, we see all too clearly the imperfections of characters. We know them for their faults as well as their strengths. As TV has evolved, the heroes of yesterday have given way to more vulnerable or damaged people as central characters: the decisive Dr Kildare gave way to the prevaricating and over-principled Dr Green or the weird and edgy Dr House; the wholesome Saint to *NYPD Blue*'s unsavoury Andy Sipowitz. For viewers, the imperfections of the characters are the source of the continuing drama. When this is the case, viewers also learn not to rush to judgement on characters. They may not be what they first appear, and certainly they are likely to change and mature as Sipowitz did. TV characters are there for the long term (if not for life), buffeted by the weekly supply of incident, and it is by no means clear how they will end up.

The industrial form of TV series production provides for this double level of narrative. The successful series will be planned meticulously in its individual incidents, so that each episode will work efficiently towards the closure of those particular incidents.**»** But the wider story arcs of the series

» Q20

and of the characters are worked out as the series develops. In the team writing that is necessary for long-running series on the American model, scriptwriters base their work on the 'bible'. This is the defining document that describes the characters and their 'back-story', their life before the series began, a mine of potential revelations as the series evolves. The nature of each character will often be defined in terms of oppositions. But their eventual finishing point, their closure, will be left open to be defined as the series develops. It will not be determined by the progress of the story itself so much as by the popularity of the character and of the series, by the success or otherwise of the performer's contract renewal negotiations. These are industrial factors that are external to the fictional world itself. There have been rare series planned with huge multi-season narrative structures, like the prestigious *Murder One* (1995–1997) or the science-fantasy series *Babylon 5*.[44] However, this last case also demonstrates the inadvisability of so doing, as the series was cancelled by the initial broadcaster Warner/PTV some time before the end of the planned structure, and the series was eventually picked up by TNT.

The lack of overall story planning in TV series may be the result of the perennial uncertainty of the TV industry, but it is nevertheless remarkable. Most stories are created by people who have an end in view to which their stories are working. It may or may not be apparent to those who are being told the story that this is the case. Their pleasures will differ depending on how clearly predictable the story is whilst it is being told. Incidents may be improvised to delay or hasten the conclusion, but most narratives are relatively efficient machines for moving towards a closure that resolves both the tensions and the initial enigmas or dilemmas. But for the TV series this is very rarely the case. It introduces an interesting randomness into television storytelling which brings it close to the patterns of everyday life, where absolute closure and sense of an ending is comparatively rare. Despite the huge number of disasters that befall soap characters, the open-ended form of narrative that tells these stories brings them close to the rhythms of the everyday.

Q17 Why do TV stories never seem to come to an end?

Q18

Why are sitcoms not as good as they used to be?

There have been plenty of unsuccessful sitcoms during the long history of the genre. It's just that we don't remember them particularly. The continuing presence of *Fawlty Towers*, *I Love Lucy* or *Roseanne* somewhere on TV makes it even harder to remember Denise Van Outen in *Babes in the Wood*, Chris Barrie in *Prince Among Men*, *Charles in Charge* or *Zoe, Duncan, Jack & Jane*. If remembered at all, such series are recalled as icons of awfulness, having failed to appeal to any section of the audience that the producers envisaged for them. Even some once-successful sitcoms fall from grace and become the kind of embarrassing memories that their former fans want to forget. *Terry and June*, the suburban British sitcom, ran for 107 episodes between 1974 and 1987, despite hostile criticism for its hackneyed plots and cosy suburban universe.

» Q35

Much TV output resists nostalgia since it is too complexly of its time.» But situation comedy is a major exception. Sitcom was invented by broadcasting. Sitcoms appeared on radio with hugely successful series like *It's That Man Again* (or *ITMA*) in the UK during the Second World War. Here the comedy was broadly farcical, full of the puns that were a feature of humour in the period, along with a broad range of catchphrases. Sitcom became more domestic and (to a significant degree) lifelike with television in the 1950s, since when it has changed remarkably little. This is one of the secrets of its success as a genre. Older sitcoms can be repeated more often and for rather longer than most types of programme. So the genre is able to quietly reinvent its history and suppress the many ideas that didn't work. Successful sitcoms from the past remain present and the unsuccessful ones quickly fade from the memory.

Gags and ideas do not make a sitcom, neither does a physical situation. The key to sitcom success is far harder to achieve. Sitcom relies on enduring conflicts between individuals who are for some reason unable to escape from their relationship. This is often a family situation, where relatives are held together by ties that are subterranean, as was the case in the classic British series *Steptoe and Son*. The aspirant Harold Steptoe was unable to leave his repellent father Albert, no matter how often he tried, failing sometimes because his father sabotaged his plans, but often because he responded to Albert's emotional blackmail. This was a successful format because the inter-generational family situation was combined with a class dimension. At this time, Britain was experiencing the decline of its traditional working class, and Albert's rag-and-bone man displayed all the worst aspects of traditional working-class men. Family relations are still the mainspring of much sitcom: series like *My Family*, *The Cosby Show* or *2 Point 4 Children* take actual families as subjects; *Friends*, *Third Rock from the Sun* or *Will & Grace* take groups who act as surrogate families. Even workplace-based sitcoms like *The Rag Trade*, *Drop the Dead Donkey* or *Peter Kay's Phoenix Nights* settle into family-like patterns.

However, the very thing that makes a sitcom work also makes it difficult to establish a new format with TV audiences. The dynamics that drive a successful sitcom are not immediately apparent to a first-time viewer. It takes time to get to know the characters and the typical interactions between them. The characters are often blinkered and obsessive, condemned to repeat their mistakes as much by their own personalities as by their situation. And repeat they do, since the essence of the format is that the characters go through all kinds of experiences and even life-threatening circumstances without undergoing any discernible transformation. Indeed, until recently, sitcoms demonstrated very little ongoing memory of previous episodes. The characters would return unscathed the following week no matter what catastrophe had befallen them. In this sense, sitcom was the most extreme example of series TV, in which there are few if any narrative developments or character evolutions across the run of a series. At the start of each episode, we find the characters of classic sitcoms in their original state, no matter how much chaos there was at the end of the previous one. They

Q18 Why are sitcoms not as good as they used to be?

live in an eternal present. Elements of memory have crept into more recent formats due both to their longevity and to the need to retain viewers. So the characters in *Friends* wedded and divorced each other. The hapless Rodney in *Only Fools and Horses* matured over the seven series and eventually married Cassandra. Perhaps this is a necessary feature of the truly long-lived sitcom. Even *I Love Lucy*, the definitive early sitcom, saw Lucy visibly pregnant and then having a screen baby – little Ricky – in 1953, in synch with the real-life birth of her son, Desi Arnaz Jnr.

However, sitcom characters do not change like soap characters, and remember little of their screen pasts. The really important activity of memory lies with the viewers. Sitcom requires that viewers are familiar with the characters and can identify their particular foibles and flashpoints: the ingenuity of Lucy's self-serving arguments and her penchant for physical comedy; the unerring stupidity of Joey Tribbiani in *Friends*; the self-importance of Hancock. These occasion more affection than irritation for the series' fans. But it remains very difficult to establish such a level of knowledge and affection, and sitcoms classically take more than one series to establish themselves, as did *Only Fools and Horses*. This is why there is a high turnover of sitcom formats, and at any one moment it seems as though there are many dismal examples and comparatively few that deserve repeated viewing.

It also contributes to the conservatism of the form: conservatism in that the format has varied relatively little over the half century since it was established by series such as *I Love Lucy*. In 1951, Lucille Ball and Desi Arnaz, her husband, negotiated to shoot their new domestic comedy series on film, using three cameras, in front of a studio audience. Up to that point, the early sitcoms had been broadcast live. *I Love Lucy*'s use of film allowed editing for pace, but maintained the contact with a live audience that is crucial for the format. *I Love Lucy* defined a pattern that still remains. The overwhelming majority of sitcoms are still half an hour long; they rely on an ensemble cast locked into unchangeable relationships; they have little or nothing in terms of a continuing narrative across a series; they use a comparatively small number of standard sets and are performed with a studio audience. The studio audience is often composed of the series' fans, who are also treated to 'warm-up' entertainers before the recording begins. In a TV industry where most drama production abandoned the studio after the 1970s, sitcom carries on regardless. There are many good reasons for this. The presence of a studio audience is vital for writers and performers to refine the timing of gags and to make sure that physical comedy works, and the laughter of collective audiences encourages laughter on the part of isolated viewers. Laughter elicits laughter. Sitcoms that do without the studio audience have less broad and physical humour, though David Brent/Ricky Gervaise's famous dance in *The Office* is perhaps the exception that proves the rule. Otherwise *The Office*, like *The Royle Family*, depends on the subtleties of seemingly innocuous remarks for its humour, which is often that of embarrassment rather than gags. The need for an audience to establish mood and performers' timing dictates the use of a studio, and the use of the studio favours the restriction to a maximum of five sets for each episode. Sitcoms tend to have a narrow repertoire of familiar spaces, like the apartment and radio station in *Frasier*, the neighbouring apartments in *Friends*, or the endless open-plan living rooms of UK sitcom. The basic set of *Sykes And A...* (1960–1965) and *2 Point 4 Children* (1991–1999), for instance, are startlingly identical. A door opens directly from the outside into a through space with stairs to one side and a door to the kitchen at the end. The Porter family and Sykes and his sister Hattie have even chosen the same place for their sofa (aka settee, couch etc). Conveniently, this is in the middle of the room, facing the studio audience and allowing people to walk behind it. Despite their wealth, the Banks family of *The Fresh Prince of Bel-Air* (1990–1996) seem to have adopted this same floor-plan.

Sitcom remains a difficult genre despite this conservatism of form. It has a high failure rate with promising formats failing to take off with audiences, and series based around hitherto successful sitcom performers, such as individuals

Q18 Why are sitcoms not as good as they used to be?

from the cast of *Seinfeld*, have not generally been successful, despite the popularity of the series. This means that at any one moment, it seems that the television is full of mediocre sitcoms, since many are being tried out and are in effect canvassing the audience for support. There are also sitcoms that appeal to one section of the audience but definitely not to everyone. This last fact might explain the long runs of *Home Improvement* (1991–1999) or *The Brittas Empire* (1991–1997), which continued despite the fact that they seemed to lack any features distinguishing them from many other discarded and forgotten formats.

Why are there so many detective series?

Detective fiction, rather than crime fiction, is a staple of TV. There are few series which have attempted to cast criminals as central characters – *The Sopranos* is a key example – but many that follow the activities of detectives. They can be private operators like Jim Rockford or Miss Marple, irascible loners within the police force like Barlow or Morse, career police officers beset by professional jealousies like Lynda La Plante's detective Jane Tennison (Helen Mirren) in *Prime Suspect*. They can be team players like Gil Grissom (William Petersen) in *CSI: Crime Scene Investigation*; ordinary police officers trying to get by, like Cagney and Lacey; time travellers like Sam Tyler (John Simm) in *Life on Mars*; or even investigators into the supernatural like Mulder and Scully in *The X-Files*. There is hardly a primetime evening that does not have some kind of detective series playing on a major channel.

Q20

Detection works well on TV because it has many aspects that suit the medium. It provides a convenient narrative of initial mystery which is eventually unravelled. It can provide a stable cast of characters along with a group of suspects and victims who change from episode to episode. It is close to precinct drama**»** in that respect, though detective dramas are less tied to a regular location. The distinctive scene of the crime is often a major feature of each episode. But the crucial aspect of detective fiction lies in how it tells its stories. Detective fiction reconstructs a story which has already happened, tracing who committed the crime and why. Detective fiction exploits a fundamental aspect of television itself. It relies on seeing and interpreting what is seen, on making evidence visible. The detective notices what others around them do not notice. The detective knows how to interpret what they see, turning observed detail into a clue and a clue into a fragment of the narrative that is waiting to be uncovered as the story unfolds. TV detective fiction, in other words, mimics the activity of watching a TV story. The detective, like the TV viewer, interprets what they see and follows the trail of clues to find the narrative that connects them together into a satisfying or truthful whole.

The evolution of the TV detective genre has followed the evolution of the TV audience since the introduction of mass entertainment TV. Initially detectives were upright police functionaries, following obvious trails of evidence and having little to do with the subtleties of human behaviour. Detectives like Fabian (in *Fabian of the Yard*) were straightforward in their search for perpetrators. By the time of *Z Cars*, detection had begun to encompass a sense of wonder or, occasionally, outrage at the vagaries of human behaviour. A detective like Columbo at the end of the 1960s adopted a more circumspect way of operating, relying for clues on what people gave away when they took his bumbling persona at face value. This was the beginning of a psychological approach to investigation, which nevertheless relied on the lack of psychological insight of those being investigated. Psychological complexity on both sides of the process arrived with series like *Cracker* in the early 1990s. Here the motives of all parties are suspect; Robbie Coltrane's Fitz has so many problems of his own that he scarcely seems equipped to figure out the motives of others, as well as being a rather implausible professor of psychology. Victims and perpetrators alike move in mysterious ways, revealing little of themselves voluntarily. It is up to us as viewers as well as the bemused police to try to make sense of the tangled motives and actions that are playing themselves out.

In every case, however, viewers were presented with images and sequences that showed things truthfully. Duplicity and lying were matters for the spoken word: the TV image remained truthful. The furthest that visual duplicity would go was the familiar technique of obscuring the vital detail in the staging of the murder that would open every episode of *Columbo*, or in the confused melee of images that formed a convenient way of drawing an audience into detective fiction episodes. By the end of the 1990s, a new approach to TV detection had developed which questioned the trustworthiness of the TV image itself: the new forensic detection series.

Series like the *CSI* franchise (*CSI: Crime Scene Investigation*; *CSI: Miami*; *CSI: New York*), or *Silent Witness* (which centres on a forensic surgeon), or the cold case series *Waking the Dead* all feature a new scientific approach to detection. Inert substances are made to speak. Scraps of physical evidence are made to yield their secrets. These series emphasise the process of going behind the visible surface of things, taking nothing for granted. Such programmes include graphic scenes of grossly damaged or putrid corpses and the macabre procedures of forensic surgeons. But, alongside these deliberate visceral shocks, these series have taken TV detective fiction to a new level by the inclusion of deliberately misleading sequences. *CSI: Crime Scene Investigation* began with a pilot episode which dramatised the misleading or even lying accounts of suspects. It also included purely speculative sequences, illustrating the hypotheses of the investigators. Some of these turned out to be wrong as well. For the first time, viewers were presented with fully dramatised sequences which did not simply avoid showing evidence (as they had done in earlier detective fictions) but were actively misleading. The contrast with the early days of *Fabian of the Yard* is huge, as it is not only the words of suspects but the television image itself that can no longer be trusted.

Both this use of deliberately misleading or dishonest visual sequences, and the forensic approach itself, work with viewers only because they are sophisticated enough to understand and appreciate them. Forensic fiction develops skills of visual literacy, encouraging an approach that looks beyond the immediately obvious and the surface. Alongside the detectives, viewers are interrogating what they see for what it can reveal rather than what it shows. They dramatise the importance of doing so, emphasising the need to weigh in judgement the status of different kinds of footage. They emphasise that everything that can be seen cannot be taken 'at face value'; that some visual sequences are more trustworthy than others; that it is necessary to sift visual evidence. These are dramas that ask their audiences to decide whether one scene can be trusted as much as another. They are dramatising the work of viewing which TV viewers (and indeed those looking at images on the Internet) now have to undertake routinely. They are forensic in the way that news bulletins are now forensic, weighing up different categories of footage from different sources, seeking the levels of truth that may lie **»** Q15, Q23 beyond the visible evidence.**»**

What is a 'precinct drama'?

'Precinct drama' is a TV term that has suddenly emerged in the jargon of writers, producers and attentive viewers and is not yet in dictionaries. Everyone in the know seems to know what it means. It is a useful term whose origins, probably American, seem obscure. Precinct drama arrived in the UK as a definition at the end of the 1990s, with the short-lived police series *City Central* being described as 'the first police precinct drama series to be commissioned by BBC Television since *Z Cars*'.[45] This claims a long tradition for the format, as *Z Cars* ran from 1962 and was not classified in this way at the time. Gareth Neame defined the term further: 'We wanted to make a precinct show along the American model of *LA Law*, *Ally McBeal* and *The West Wing*, which combined the economy of the studio with the high production values of a location shoot.'[46] Both *LA Law* and *Ally McBeal* were set in the offices of a law firm, and *The West Wing* was a fantasy of a Democrat White House administration. Neame referred to another show using the term: 'an original precinct drama that focuses on the real lives of ordinary working people who found themselves below stairs in an English country house in the mid 19th century',[47] and the writer David Edgar has referred to '[Steven] Bochco's reinvention of precinct drama in legal and police series like *LA Law* and *NYPD Blue*'.[48] Other obvious precinct dramas are those set in hospitals like the BBC's *Casualty* and *Holby City*, or *ER*, *Gray's Anatomy* and *Chicago Hope*.

Precinct dramas are long-running series set in organised institutions like police stations, hospitals, law firms, the White House and, so it seems, even the English country house. Most of the action is confined to those locations, although they do not seem cramped. The 'economy of the studio', referred to by Neame, does not imply that the sets look obvious or cheap. A major part of the initial production investment for a precinct drama is spent on the construction of elaborate standing sets whose meticulous details and 'real working parts' are matched by their flexibility. The hospital precinct series *ER* is famous for its sets, which enable both the removal of walls to facilitate shooting and the trademark 360-degree camera movements, swooping round the prone bodies of the unfortunate victims of accidents and shootings as the ER team battle to save them. The *ER* set is extravagant, and is as much like a real hospital as possible. So it is no wonder that most of the action in any one episode takes place within it. The use of these complex standing sets has three advantages. They are designed for shooting, so they speed up the process which is essential for a series that is on-screen (as many US precinct dramas are) for more than twenty hour-long episodes a year. This is the real 'economy of the studio'. It equally allows the actors to feel at home within the spaces, increasing the sense of reality in their performances. It also defines the series, bestowing an instantly recognisable trademark look.

A precinct is a particular kind of institution: one that brings together a working group of people with a steady through-put of individuals whose problems and dramatic stories must be sorted out by that working group. Hence the preponderance of precincts that deal with law-breakers and the sick. This combination provides almost infinite possibilities for storytelling. The relatively stable group of medics, lawyers and police relate to each other in a sustained way, working through issues of workplace culture (internal politics and workplace romances), work/life relations (they usually neglect their loved ones in favour of the job); loyalty, disloyalty and corruption; ambition, commitment and difficult moral decisions. They are familiar figures for the audience, growing in stature as the series continues. Their developing relationships, both sustained and broken, form the dramatic bedrock of the series. *ER* fans saw the evolution of John Carter through some 250 episodes from a callow intern to the status of medical guru and eventually a medical volunteer in Africa. They saw his failed relationships, including one with Abby Lockhart, who herself worked her way up from nurse to doctor. Long-running precinct dramas like *ER* and *NYPD Blue* have been through numerous changes of lead characters, but, as is clear from their title sequences, their star cast is anything up to a dozen people. Some, like George Clooney in *ER*, might seem to dominate once their movie career takes off on the back of their series fame, but the ensemble is all. The series depends on the development of this large group of characters and not on one who predominates. The emphasis is on the plausibility of their dilemmas and the way that they succeed or fail to grow as people during the series.

Every week the precinct drama's characters confront the problems that come through their doors. People arrive with their crimes and their injuries, as victims or perpetrators or sometimes both. They offer the potential for emotional commitment on the part of both the precinct regulars and their viewers. Every week provides a new emotional roller-coaster as a new kind of difficulty and a new attitude to adversity is demonstrated by these new cases. The characters engage with these people and their problems, judging them and taking moral stances, whilst they go about their work. It is sometimes clear to the viewer that the police or doctors are making mistakes, with their judgement clouded by events in their professional or personal lives with which we are all too familiar. Equally, they sometimes have to break the rules to help someone, or fall back on professional reserve in order to deal with the overwhelming tide of demands that come their way. The precinct drama, therefore, has it all. It has familiarity of characters; it has a familiar situation; and it has constant novelty.

A successful precinct drama is a major undertaking. There are so many stories going on that it can all get quite confusing. The shock of the arrival of a new and defining form of precinct drama in the USA in 1981, *Hill Street Blues*, was palpable. Here was a precinct drama, set in this case in a police station house, which had not only multiple characters but multiple stories as well. Characters had their own stories but also, crucially, played major roles in the stories of others, and the stories weaved into each other. Even more radically, each episode in the first series of the show simply advanced those various stories. There was

Q20 What is a 'precinct drama'?

nothing that began, developed and ended within the space of a one-hour episode. The series was a critical success, but not a ratings success. Nevertheless, the commissioning network ABC, in need of some prestige, continued with it. The producer, Steven Bochco, made one crucial concession: each episode would contain a narrative strand that was completed within its allotted span of one day.

Hill Street Blues set a pattern that continues in series like Bochco's subsequent *NYPD Blue* or *ER*. Both formats have produced a decade's worth of episodes at a rate of between eighteen and twenty-four episodes a year.[49] A typical episode of *NYPD Blue* can contain some five or six storylines. The penultimate, twenty-first, episode of the first series shows how complicated their interaction can be.[50] Greg Medavoy storms into the station having discovered his wife in flagrante with her lover. He tells the station receptionist Donna (they have been flirting for most of the series), who offers him a bed for the night. On his way to pick up a suspect, he and his partner Martinez are stuck in traffic and Medavoy catches the eye of the irate black driver in the next lane. Medavoy's mood is such that he does not look away; the man gets aggressive, pulls a gun and Martinez shoots him dead. The race dimension is central from the start,[51] as is the fact that Medavoy's personal life has momentarily but tragically affected how he relates to people. The precinct force begin to investigate the scene, but are beaten back by a near riot in which Detective Janice Licalsi is seized by a group of men. Her ex-lover, Detective Kelly, tries to comfort her, but she is still, as throughout the series, haunted by the fact she shot a mafia figure who was trying to blackmail her. Kelly sends her to an old friend, a Catholic priest, for advice. Kelly protects Martinez from the police internal investigation men and, with his partner Sipowicz, begins to investigate the shooting. Sipowicz indulges in some of his trademark intimidation of suspects, and Kelly, less typically, undertakes some intimidation of his own. A pushy TV reporter alleges (correctly as it turns out) that the gun toted by Martinez's victim was not loaded. He threatens to reveal this in his next on-the-hour bulletin, and

Kelly demonstrates graphically, by threatening him, how difficult it is to tell whether a gun is loaded or not. Licalsi talks to the priest and, as a result, confesses to the station chief that she shot a mobster illegally. Kelly tries to sort things out for her, unsuccessfully, and Sipowicz takes time out to attend an Alcoholics Anonymous meeting where he encounters a criminal he had given a break to earlier in the series. Eventually the gun in the Martinez/Medavoy shooting is turned in, and the internal investigators declare it a 'righteous shooting'. The episode ends with Licalsi being led from the precinct house under arrest and being mobbed by the waiting press.

This episode combines a number of storylines. The Martinez/Medavoy shooting begins and ends within the episode, but that has been caused by the ongoing problems of one of the regular characters. Its second storyline concludes Licalsi's story, which has run since the beginning of the series some twenty episodes previously, and is one that focuses on the morality of police work. The episode significantly develops three further stories: Medavoy's marriage and flirtation with Donna; Sipowicz's struggle with alcoholism; and the story of the TV reporter who has been trying to blackmail the police into allowing his then-novel mini-cam into the inside of the precinct house. So there are in fact five active storylines within this one episode, each contributing to the others. There is also material that relates to other storylines as well. These include: the recipient of Sipowicz's generosity, who was an incidental character from an earlier episode; Kelly's relationship with Robin Wirkus; and Sipowicz's problematic one with Sylvia Costas from the DA's office. These would be picked up only by devoted viewers. In this episode, Kelly is constantly on the move between incidents, trying to make things come out all right, but he is not the protagonist of any story as he often is in other episodes of this first series.

The plotting of these stories is a complex and collective operation. In a series of meetings, the scriptwriting team (most of whom are called 'producer' or 'executive producer' on the opening credits) develop the long-

Q20 What is a 'precinct drama'?

running stories around each character, the potential for interaction between them, and the possible candidates for the stories that are completed in one episode. An outline plan is worked out for the series, so the most appropriate single-episode incidents are married with the long-running plots. In the case of this episode, this combination provides a deep thematic contrast between the righteous shooting by Martinez of someone threatening a fellow officer with a gun, and the illegal shooting of the mobster by Licalsi. Equally a thematic parallel emerges between Sipowicz's attempt to sort his life out and Licalsi's decision to come to terms with her conscience. The process of planning and the subsequent drafting and redrafting can produce a complex interrelation between stories at the thematic level as well as ensuring that action in one story affects actions in others. This process continues as individual writers or writing pairs develop a particular storyline into more detailed scripts. These separate sub-scripts are then married together into an episode script by a specially delegated writer. In contrast to this complex writing process, the shooting is a relatively simple affair. The actors know their characters and the main location; the crew are regulars and the directors are constrained by the overall trademark visual style of the series. Very occasionally, this routine is deliberately disrupted to keep everyone and everything on their toes. *ER* famously did one episode as a live broadcast[52] and had Quentin Tarantino as director of another.

Precinct dramas are sometimes confused with soaps, or are seen as part of a 'soapisation' of TV drama. However, they are distinct from soap operas because they have a different balance of regular and temporary characters. A soap is dominated by its regulars and temporary incomers are sparingly used. In a precinct drama, the regular characters constantly react to the influx of new problems, and this provides the impetus of the series. Precinct drama also occupies a different place in the schedule to a soap. The budget is far higher and the number of episodes far lower. The use of cliffhanger endings is much more sparing, and the progress of character development is more sustained. Soap characters are prone to forgetting chunks of their previous lives, and to wild swings in their characterisation. Precinct drama conforms to a more theatrical tradition of coherent characterisation and slow development. Precinct drama is the drama of stress and the workplace, whereas the soap is the drama of worry and the home.

Q21 Why are there so many soap operas?

There are so many soap operas on TV because they suit the medium so well. Soap operas are overwhelmingly domestic in setting, and put relationships at their heart. They provide regular, even daily, episodes involving familiar characters in a serial form, with plotlines carried on from episode to episode. Soap characters regularly face new crises and are changed by them. They remember their pasts, and, in a few cases, manage to learn from them. Jostein Gripsrud has pointed out that soap characters inhabit a kind of parallel world. They live their lives at the same pace as those of their viewers, so that the daily or weekly visit to their world shows that it has moved on by the same period of time. Soap characters live in our time, growing old with their viewers. But they live a different kind of life and, as all soaps are different, the character of those lives differs remarkably between cultures and even within one national broadcasting system. In soap opera, events take place that are frequently beyond the scope of most people's lives. They are often exaggerations of real-life dilemmas. The ordinary soap character will go through more traumas in a few years than most people could suffer in a whole lifetime. Soaps dramatise: they are fiction. Soaps exaggerate because they are melodrama, using clearly defined emotions to explore complex moral issues. But soaps are also mundane, involving familiar characters and an everyday timescale. Soaps have the rhythm of everyday life, but the narrative range of fiction.

Traditionally, the target audience of TV soaps was presumed to be female, the archetypal 'housewife at home'. Their concentration on emotional dilemmas was targeted at women in post-war societies where an emotional division of labour between men and women was assumed. However, as emotional concerns have become more central to culture as a whole,**»** the core audience of many soaps is nowadays more diverse. In particular, soaps provide many early adolescents, both male and female, with a key means of learning about the world of adults. They also attract a

» Q7

more knowing, ironic audience. Drawing on the work of Ien Ang, Andrea Milwood Hargrave[53] identifies four types of attitude to soaps: the fans who are committed to their choice of soap; the ironic viewers who watch regularly but believe that soaps are rubbish; the non-committed; and the dismissive. Her team's research, based on 2,100 detailed questionnaires, established that the fans tended to be 'mainly female, tabloid readers [with] no [university] degree, tending to be younger and from lower social class' whereas the ironic viewers tended to be older, and men predominate over women. The non-committed had the same profile as the overall population of the UK, but the majority of the dismissive were 'men, the oldest group, high proportion of ABs and broadsheet readers'. Importantly, the survey established that around half the audience members surveyed discussed the issues raised in soap operas with family members or work colleagues.[54] This research confirms that UK soap operas have a complex relationship with their audiences and are still subject to a degree of class- and gender-based cultural prejudice. This prejudice arises from their combination of the everyday with dramas of the heart and a necessary level of fictional hyperbole.

The exact combination of fictional exaggeration and everyday rhythm differs with every soap. The USA invented the term 'soap opera' to describe daytime radio serials of the 1930s, which were sponsored and often even produced by soap manufacturers like Proctor and Gamble. The term 'opera' is a disparaging one, indicating both overblown emotional temperature and, sarcastically, the low cultural level of many such serials. The radio serial format was quickly adopted for TV, and many of the US daytime soaps have a hospital setting, like *As the World Turns*, which has run on CBS since 1956.[55] Social settings, class and race issues are kept to a minimum, with inter-character emotional tangles and life-threatening situations forming the basis of the dramas. Peak-time soap operas in the USA, which had significant success in the 1980s with series like *Dallas* and *Dynasty*, have some of the same characteristics, but opted for a definite social setting: the

Q21 Why are there so many soap operas?

fantasy world of the super-rich who nevertheless seemed able to inhabit the same family house, no matter how tense relations might be getting. Romantic entanglements and the family are the main preoccupation of US soaps as they are of soaps in every context.

Soap operas in the UK have a reputation for more concrete and realistic settings. Certainly they are used as a means of informal public education by the BBC, working through attitudes to teenage parenting, abortion and adoption in an early evening series like *EastEnders*. The familiarity of soap characters makes the genre particularly useful in this respect. Audiences may well relate in one way to novel characters in issue-based drama series or single dramas, and in a different way to familiar soap characters facing the same dilemmas. UK soaps have tended to take a geographical location as their base, with *Coronation Street* leading the way since 1960 with its 'typical' Northern terrace with a pub and corner shop. *EastEnders* is centred on Albert Square in one of the poorer parts of the east of London, and Channel 4's *Brookside* (1982–2003) physically adapted a real development of new houses as its basic set, allowing it to show an ill-assorted group of Northerners trying to settle into a new area. British TV soaps tend to incorporate substantial references to everyday rhythms, and will include genuinely mundane moments like shopping and cooking. The amounts of these vary according to the ratings fortunes of a soap. Spectacular accidents and controversial issues feature more prominently at times when producers and broadcasters believe that audience interest is fading. In 1993, ITV's flagging *Emmerdale* killed off a substantial number of cast regulars when a plane crashed on its rural community. All soaps mix familiarity, repetition and routine, which are the key features of the everyday, with high drama and shock revelations, which decidedly are not. On both counts they have been condemned as rubbish, both for being boringly everyday and for being outrageously unrealistic. The combination of the routine and drama, the familiar and the exceptional, is the basis of their appeal.

Yet even 'realistic' soaps develop a curious parallel

world of their own. Where the teenagers of *Hollyoaks* seem totally at home with the culture of mobile phones and SMS texting, for a long time the characters of *EastEnders* hardly seemed to know that the technology existed. Long-time regular Ian Beale showed off his new mobile in November 2006, making him probably the last person in Britain of his type to get one. Where instant communication of gossip by texting often drives forward *Hollyoaks* plots, *EastEnders* seems to prefer face-to-face gossip and speculation as its typical mode. Indeed, *EastEnders* avoids many of the current problems of inner-city Britain. It is set in the fictional area of Walford, where young people looking for affordable London housing should go immediately. It is a vibrant local community with good transport links (including the tube) that has totally escaped gentrification despite its elegant Victorian terraces. Walford is a place of pubs and clubs, shops and cafes, but there is not a home-improver's skip, artists' studio or new media outfit in sight, as there is in every similar area of London. Oddly, *EastEnders* deals with social issues but does not represent the vibrant – or, more accurately, edgy – world of the modern metropolis. There are no beggars haunting the Walford cashpoints because the characters don't make much use of ATMs there; Albert Square has no discarded KFC boxes because Walford is the one urban enclave in Britain that the multiples have not colonised. If they want fast food, they visit the cafe or chip shop rather than scoff a kebab or a burger on the run. There are none of London's new-wave immigrants: no former Yugoslavs, no Roma, no Nigerians, no Somalis, no Polish builders. You are unlikely to encounter a mugger in Walford urgently in need of some way of financing their next hit; the typical unpleasant street encounter is with a drunk stumbling from the Vic, intent on some very personal act of vengeance. The reality of even a realistic soap is one of a particular parallel universe: close to ours but not the same. If it were, they would be watching soaps on TV, which would be the ultimate transgression of the boundary between our everyday world and their parallel one.

Other soap cultures adopt different tactics. The

Q21 Why are there so many soap operas?

Australian soaps like *Neighbours* and *Home and Away* are set in a suburbia where people often struggle to make ends meet, combining aspects of the US and UK approaches. The huge industry of Brazil and Mexico has evolved another distinctive approach: the telenovela. Instead of the Anglo-Saxon open-ended series which can last half a century and more, the typical novela is planned to last for up to two years' worth of five daily episodes a week. So the novela has an end in view towards which it can move its characters. This allows writers to work towards a final moment of punishment or redemption for the characters, and enables them to provide a distinctive contemporary feeling to some of its central themes. Brazilian novelas often have a strong class dimension alongside the main soap preoccupations with family and romance ('poor girl marries rich man and is disowned' is a popular basic situation).

The main Brazilian producer-broadcaster TV Globo has for many years run three novelas every evening. This produces a set of distinctive formats: a novela evening will encompass one series set in the colonial past, a second dealing with teen issues and a third with a controversial theme like corruption or human cloning, possibly with a crime-investigation theme. So in the Brazilian market the novela form spreads to encompass aspects of other genres, largely taking the place occupied in the US system

» Q20

by precinct dramas.**»** Novelas have a substantial export market, unlike British soaps. Brazil's *Isaura the Slave Girl* (*Escrava Isaura*) in 1976 and Mexico's *The Rich Cry Too* (*Los ricos tambien lloran*) in 1979 being early examples. As

» Q9

a reaction against the globalisation of TV,**»** local versions of successful novela formats are being produced in large TV markets like Russia which have hitherto shown dubbed episodes of the originals. The Russian version of Colombian *Betty La Fea* (*Betty the Ugly*) was *Ne Rodis Krasivoi* (*Don't Be Born Beautiful*). It was one of the most successful shows on Russian TV in 2005 with a thirty-seven per cent audience share.[56] As *Ugly Betty*, the US version was played more clearly for comedy, although it was made for a one-hour slot rather than the more usual sitcom half-hour. The TV in Betty's home is constantly tuned to a Latino channel showing novelas, and the sultry eroticism and melodramatic twists of character are clearly offered for further laughs. Channel 4 in the UK bought this US version rather than making a local adaptation, and trailed the first episode as 'the new sitcom', scheduling it in the Friday slot that was for many years the home of *Friends*, *Will & Grace* and other imported US sitcoms. Nevertheless, *Ugly Betty* has a different plot structure to a sitcom, with a strong serial development from week to week like its source novela. In terms of the genres of US TV, *Ugly Betty* has more in common with a series like *Desperate Housewives*, which has never been promoted as a sitcom despite its comedic elements and pervasive music underscore using pizzicato violins to indicate 'quirky comedy', a feature it shares with *Ugly Betty*. The example of the career of *Betty La Fea* clearly shows the problems of transferring an example of a strong genre (the telenovela) to another culture.》 It equally shows that the novela is genre that shares many of the characteristics of the soap opera in its daily schedule and its narrative patterns, but extends, in its home markets, to encompass aspects of other drama genres as well.

The near-daily scheduling of many soaps has developed a whole industry of satellite publications and fan activity. Magazines like *Soap Opera Digest* in the USA have proliferated since the beginning of the 1980s, and soap opera updates are a feature of daily newspapers and weekly women's magazines in the UK. The lives of soap actors provide a further focus for magazine and website speculation. Soap operas were among the first TV formats to develop a more dispersed relationship with their viewers, ranging more widely than the moment of viewing of a broadcast episode. Reality TV has built upon ideas of seriality developed by soap operas, and this is one component of the success of this new genre.》 The parallel world of each soap opera relies on broadcast TV for its continuing relationship with its viewers. Soap characters have a history which they remember well, as do their viewers. This distinguishes soaps from sitcoms which

Q21 Why are there so many soap operas?

repeat variations on an unchanging set of interpersonal relations.» In the soap opera, viewers can see, discuss and be involved with the changes that characters undergo because of their changing circumstances. Soap operas tell us that people can change; sitcoms tell us that they will not.

Whatever happened to the single TV play?

Once upon a time, TV was sharply divided into three categories. There were uplifting or experimental single dramas, serials consisting of one story told over a number of episodes, and the repetitive formulaic series together with their low-budget relatives, the soap operas. Over time, the various forms have exchanged some characteristics, but the judgements of quality which rate the single over the series continue to be expressed. Many older TV professionals regret the passing of the 'single drama' on TV, which created such classics as *Marty* in the USA and *Cathy Come Home* and *Lena Oh My Lena* in the UK. But these were rarities, even at the time of their creation. They were the moments of prestige TV,» where the limits of the medium were being pushed and something of perceived cultural and artistic merit was created. Behind the belief in the single drama lies the view that fundamental creativity lies in the original and unique object rather than in a series or in a structure of variation within repetition. Even in the golden age of the single drama, the 1950s and 1960s, TV series were the norm.

The single drama lives on as an ideal, however, and still exists in the form of particular one-off fiction events or the mini-series. It is particularly suited to the reconstruction of key historic events or the anticipation of future dystopias like *The Day Britain Stopped* (BBC Two, 2003). The single drama resembles the most valued commodity in our moving-image culture, the cinematic feature film, and some have effectively become 'films' through cinema release.[57] In Europe, this crossover is the basis of a fruitful investment and collaboration between cinema and TV. The single drama is easier to show again, to study and perhaps to recall, than a long series of similar episodes. Despite the cultural credibility that the single drama form still has, it remains a rarity on primetime TV. In a competitive medium, the single drama can be seen as a waste of resources – not of financial resources so much as resources of the imagination. Why go to the trouble of inventing characters and situations and then discard them after one single outing? TV is an everyday medium, full of variations on existing themes rather than constant bold innovation.**»** So a single drama that has any merit deserves further exploration of its characters and their dilemmas. Series dominate because series fit how people use TV.

» Q30

Beginnings and ends are a real problem for TV drama. A beginning means that fresh characters, situations and dynamics have to be introduced. Endings mean that a whole fictional universe is being discarded.**»** Both are difficult for a medium that thrives on both familiarity and competition. Familiarity comes with the everyday domestic role of TV, and competition with the burgeoning number of channels as well as other entertainment and information media from Playstation and X-Box to mobile phones, MySpace and YouTube. Creating and launching a TV format is a risky activity, especially in the USA where pilots are made and discarded, and even commissioned series have to survive a cull in the middle of their first season. It is not a long period in which to establish characters and situations with an audience.

» Q17

The form of the TV series evolved very quickly. The first formats took a constant character or group and placed them in a situation where recurring conflict was inevitable. So, in the late 1950s version, Robin Hood and his men would be forever in conflict with the Sheriff of Nottingham and other henchmen of the evil King John; the good King Richard would, Godot-like, be endlessly expected but never appear; and Maid Marian would continue to be in jeopardy. Robin's men consisted of a core group of sharply defined outlaws (Friar Tuck, 'Little' John, Will Scarlett, etc, who on occasion would dispute Robin's leadership decisions), along with a wider band of extras. The format could generate numerous weekly stories along one or other of the lines of conflict, as well as weekly scenes of group solidarity and humour. It might have been a formula, but it was a potent one. And it threw the emphasis away from the self-contained story that would be provided by a movie or a novel. Instead, it provided a new balance of storytelling, where character familiarity was as important as the weekly narrative tensions.

Narratives work on the basis of an initial revelation of their subject, a situation that is disrupted or a problem to be resolved. Characters are introduced, already in conflict or soon to be so. After this initial phase, the conflict or problem is explored, with protagonists being delayed, diverted or frustrated in finding a resolution. The eventual ending sees the conflict resolved, and a new state of equilibrium for the characters, or at least those who are left. In effect, the early form of the TV series, like *Robin Hood*, introduced two levels of narrative, one weekly and one for eternity. The weekly narrative was played out in each episode. The Sheriff would launch a search for Robin's hideout or would hold Maid Marian hostage, and by the end of the episode be frustrated by Robin's daring and ingenuity. Or again, a potential new member of the outlaws would come forward, who might be genuine or might be a spy. Or a raid on a group of overfed priests or repressive tax-gatherers would lead to complications. Each story would be resolved by the end of the episode by the return to the initial equilibrium: Robin in his forest hideaway, basking in his moral rectitude and awaiting the return of King Richard; the Sheriff fuming, his rapacious intent frustrated for the moment.

The second, eternal, level of narrative is one of familiarity and repetition. It lies in the shifting dynamic of the recurring characters and takes place as the episodes accumulate. Each challenge to Robin is distinct: he is the same man but his judgements can differ, particularly in relation to circumstances involving Maid Marian. His group of outlaws respond predictably but with characteristic humour, overconfidence or downright incompetence. They are held in the perpetual middle of some larger narrative, larger probably than the series itself. For they clearly had a past which drove them to the status of outlaws, and their expectation of the restoration of the good King Richard implies the eventual end of that status, perhaps retirement in some medieval equivalent of suburbia, tending their allotment strips in peace. In other words, the second narrative of the series is one of almost infinite middle, where the mechanisms of delay, diversion and frustration are multiplied until they become the very condition of the characters' being. There clearly was something before their current state, and perhaps there will be something after, but for viewers they are held in a present of delay where we can get to know them better. This is one of the essential pleasures of following a story: the development and the testing of character through the onward flow of events.»

» Q17

Indeed the mechanisms of delay are the real source of pleasure in narrative. There can be excitement and anticipation at the beginning, and a sense of satisfaction at the ending, but both are minor compared with the twists of the middle, the deceptions and revelations, the risks and miscalculations. The excitement felt at the beginning of a narrative is in large part one of savouring the possibilities offered by the situation, its relevance to public or personal life or its recognisable elements (genre, star, period etc). And the ending, though resolving tensions (and so a necessary part of narrative), is always tinged with regret at leaving the characters or indeed at leaving the situation with so many possibilities left unexploited. Many an unsatisfying film is unsatisfying because it did not exploit the richness of its initial premise, or left us still intrigued by its characters.

When it was first developed, the TV series established a means of avoiding such frustrations. It provided a weekly narrative with its satisfying resolution, but equally made clear that this was just one episode in a much larger conflict which provided its second narrative. The second narrative seemed to be 'all middle' but in fact tended to imply a state before the arrival of the characters, a back-story that had brought them to this particular state. As a series continues, more elements of this back-story become clear as the character develops, and can lead to sometimes climactic revelations such as that of the first name of Inspector Morse, which hinted at a motivating past for the character who was at that point being 'killed off' by his creators. The future ending is, like all futures, uncertain. However, its outlines can be dimly perceived as a state of equilibrium that the characters themselves will sometimes ruefully discuss as a goal that they doubt they will attain. This second narrative could be seen as that of life itself: where death is inevitable but everything else is uncertain, and change is accompanied by the return of familiar characters and situations. In this way, the simplest TV series provides a philosophical perspective which reconciles its viewers with one of the fundamental facts of existence. The only certainty of life is that it will end.

Is there too much sport on TV?

In the days of limited broadcast channels, big sporting occasions would mean that schedules were cleared to accommodate them. The Olympics still tend to lead to a wholesale suspension of normal schedules, and major football fixtures can still force soaps to move over to accommodate them occasionally. In the past this was common, and this produced the complaint that there was 'too much' sport on TV, often fuelled by household divisions on gender lines: the males wanted to watch the sport, the females were shut out of their habitual viewing as a result. Multiple channels and multiple sets in households have tended to reduce this problem, as well as the emergence of sport, along with movies, as a key means of promoting cable or satellite subscription services.

For sport and TV were made for each other. Sport is popular. Many events sell out well in advance, and results are the subject of everyday conversation. Sports events demand live coverage, as sport is supremely of the moment and is rarely predictable in its outcomes. Most sports have a competitive structure that lends them to a clear narrative of challenge, success and failure. Sports events have a relatively predictable duration and have established fan bases. All these factors made sport a natural TV subject from the beginnings of the medium.

Nevertheless, TV has not left sport as it found it. TV has altered the nature of many sports events to make them fit scheduling patterns and narrative formats. The traditional football habit of replaying drawn cup finals has given way to the penalty shoot-out. This responds to the need for a narrative that ends within one TV afternoon or evening. Cricket has added one-day, limited-over matches to the traditional format of an event that can, in the case of test matches, last to a maximum of five days. Every sport with major TV coverage has evolved super-finals, gladiatorial events like the Superbowl or the European Cup Winners Cup which become regular TV events and draw in even those with little interest in the game.

In effect, TV has extended the narrative of sport and recreated it as a TV series, with each match or event acting as an episode in a larger ongoing structure.**»** Each win is just a step towards a greater goal, and each loss recoverable through better performance in the future. Even though each match is utterly engrossing as it unrolls, and the disappointments of losing are real enough, this larger narrative structure gives hope for the future even to supporters of the losing teams or competitors right up until the culmination of the series. A nationally based series can often be the gateway to a further international competition, so a success at a national level can lead to a further international narrative. Some sports concentrate this structure into a short period like the two weeks of Wimbledon tennis, although there is a persistent attempt to create Wimbledon as the culmination of a longer series of world tennis competitions. Athletics and related sports already have such a long-form narrative structure in the Olympics, held every four years and embracing every sport known to TV (apart from snooker and darts), and several more as well. By organising sports into a clear structure of episodes and larger series, TV has remade sport in its own image, giving it the temporal and narrative structure of a long-running TV drama series.

As well as creating long narrative series from sports, television has transformed sports by giving them increased visibility. It has made sports highly visible in modern culture and has given them their characteristic forms of visualisation. As a result, many sports have become professionalised, and sporting heroes have become celebrities. These celebrities have an important narrative function in TV coverage.**»** They provide a further level of narrative beyond that of the match and the series by providing forms of personal drama that run alongside. So the career arc of a David Beckham or a perceived conflict between two stars can provide an additional set of story concerns to that of game and series. This element of characterisation is particularly marked with individual competitive sports like athletics, and is often combined, at international level, with a blatant national bias. The

Q23 Is there too much sport on TV?

established stars of the domestic arena become national champions. However, the increased international trade in players in sports like football is beginning to complicate this, as international matches can sometimes set national teammates against each other.

TV has brought a mobile and analytic visibility to sports. Sports before television were designed to be viewed from a fixed spectatorial position, and some seats (where they were provided) were better than others. TV has gradually constructed complex composite views, which bring together **»** **Q16** all kinds of perspective.**»** The spectatorial point of view is still the basic view for the televising of most sports events: viewing from a raised position at a distance that gives a general perspective and so differs from the fixed view of any participant or spectator. From that starting point, TV has had to work out a scheme of points of view for each sport, gradually adding more adventurous angles so that the composite views now offered are extremely complicated. Any major event will be covered from a large number of angles, but a set of overall decisions will have been taken. These cover the scale and range of the shots, for example: how close to the action will spectators be brought; will there be close-ups of the players; will there be cutaways to individuals in the crowd, to the support crews or managers; will there be shots from above the action; are there opportunities to place cameras right inside the action, in the helmets of participants, cricket stumps etc. Equally important are the decisions about the sound perspectives to be used. Coverage of sports depends on the kinds of sounds that are available. Do we hear the crowd as a whole or will the sound of people in particular positions be brought forward so that we hear their individual voices? The sounds of team players can now be made audible, allowing individual grunts and instructions to be heard. Either option has its problems: some crowds can deliver racist taunts, and some players can enter into vivid arguments with the referee. The choice of sound perspectives determines how much, if at all, the TV viewers of a sport are made aware of the event as a social gathering with wider implications than just the game and result.

The TV visibility of sport extends beyond providing a composite view of the event as it unfolds. Action is easily missed even by the keenest of spectators, and it is often unclear what precisely went on. TV sports departments have long been at the forefront of technological innovation in TV, seizing on any new advance as a means of extending its reach into the event. So TV coverage of major sports incorporates a number of devices which expand and contract the time of the live event even as it unfolds. There are instant replays, often with instantaneous graphic analysis of various kinds to highlight aspects of the action; there are fearsome displays of statistics overlaying the image; displays of other relevant information including biographies of players or timings in relation to a series of established records. There are even hypothetical reconstructions of action based on the necessarily partial view that the most extravagant coverage of action nevertheless provides. The use of these explanatory structures differs between broadcasters, and can be puzzling to those who do not know the particular habits of a TV culture. One feature of commentary on international matches is the audible frustration of commentators who themselves are having to work out what shots are being displayed by the local

Q26 broadcast feed and why.**》** A few sports are not amenable to this baroque visual treatment. Horse races are relatively intractable for TV as the races themselves are over in a few minutes and the run-up to each race yields little in terms of visual complexity.

In all sports, however, visibility and recapitulation are not enough. A crucial component of the visibility of all sports on TV is the activity of commentary. Sporting action alone is fleeting and needs a level of technical knowledge and connoisseurship to appreciate it. Crowd interaction and interpersonal induction by parents and peers can provide this for those who attend matches and events. However, for the TV audience, elucidation is always a problem, hence the ubiquitous role of the commentators and the analytic frameworks. Commentators are everywhere in sports coverage, and individuals can, as Karen Lury perceptively

Q23 Is there too much sport on TV?

points out, come to exemplify the spirit of the sport, more even than the participants:

> For the listening audience, the commentators' voices, their pitch, pace, resonance and expression, become entwined with the way in which various sports are enjoyed on television ... The voice, therefore, provides more than description and, over time, becomes an implicated and familiar part of the 'play' of the rhythms, textures, tones and pace of the televised experience of individual sports.[58]

So the high-pitched hysteria of Murray Walker exemplifies Formula One, and Northern accents are inseparable from snooker.

Commentary is more than description: it develops the essential structure of TV sport, bringing out the full complexities of the narratives involved, and even breaking down the very images of the events themselves by subjecting them to relentless analysis. Pre-match discussions set up expectations that will be fulfilled or dashed by the action. Recapitulations during and after the action explore what has happened through the use of replays and analysed footage. **TV has brought a forensic visibility to sport.** Any action is mulled over and analysed for all its potential meanings and consequences. Commentators speculate freely on the possible motives of a player, the possible feelings of competitors as they struggle with each other for supremacy. This reflects the kind of conversations that might be taking place amongst the connoisseurs in the viewing audience.[59] But it has a vastly expanded repertoire of reference, from the ability to subject the image to physical interrogation to databanks of statistics and examples from previous actions.

Sport has been, along with news, in the forefront of technological innovation in the TV industry because of its insistent need to analyse and explain. In the recent introduction of reconstructions, sports coverage demonstrates its forensic abilities. The reconstructions

» Q19

admit that the camera viewpoints are partial; that any specific camera angle has its blind spots; that the particular placing of bodies can obscure what happens in the dubious tackle, the obscurity of the scrum or the exact placing of foot or ball. Reconstructions of how a tackle happened or the exact trajectory of a ball hit by bat or racket are now a commonplace of sports coverage. They are no different from the forensic reconstructions of bullet wounds in the *CSI* series, or the news explanations of global events. All forensic reconstructions show that the image is the start of a process of analysis rather than a simple proof. That process of analysis is a new stage in the development of audio-visual literacy.

This increasing prevalence of analysis in sports coverage has coincided with the growth of participation by women in the connoisseurship of sports, like football, which have traditionally had a male image. To assert a causal relationship between these two facts would be excessive, just as it is to assert a causal relationship between the

Q11

excessive consumption of TV and food.» It is possible to assert, however, that the increased cultural centrality of sports as a subject of everyday conversation does result from its domestication by TV. Sport has been transformed by the long process of bringing it into the home which TV has undertaken. The price of that domestication has been the narrativisation of sport and the relentless increase in forensic analysis to which it is subjected. It has brought money of all kinds into many sports, often fuelled by the possibilities for gambling on results. It has also, possibly, made it easier for the old gender divide around sport to begin to break down.

Q23 Is there too much sport on TV?

What is 'reality TV'?

» Q25

Reality TV grew out of documentary, but has become a distinct TV genre. It combines ordinary people into a situation which takes them out of their everyday life, either by setting them a challenge» or by constructing an entirely artificial situation that often uses elements drawn from game shows. In such formats, real people perform versions of themselves over which they believe they have some kind of control. There is an entertainment aspect of reality TV which provides much of its appeal, both for viewers and for participants. Documentary, by contrast, involves the discussion of issues, the analysis of situations or some kind of sustained interrogation of people by the film and its makers. Documentary makes a sustained attempt to portray people in their everyday lives, and for that reason many people are increasingly reluctant to participate in one. Documentary normally involves sustained narration, whereas reality TV shows often tend to repeat key moments and to recap regularly on previous events, an inheritance from their entertainment roots. Documentary has some overall explanatory intent, whereas reality TV lets people get on with it, and leaves the viewer to puzzle out what the status and significance of their behaviour might be.

Some definitions of reality TV stretch to include infotainment like *Changing Rooms* or *What Not to Wear*, in which the role of the presenters is insistent and consistent week on week. Compared to Trinny and Susanna, the makeover candidates play a secondary role. Such over-broad definitions miss the novelty of the genre. More properly, reality TV includes the many formats that foreground ordinary people doing relatively ordinary things like learning to drive or taking on a challenging job (as in docusoaps like *Driving School* or *Airport*); or being confronted with a challenge to their behaviour or beliefs

» Q25

(as in *Brat Camp*);» or simply being placed in some kind of artificial, pressured environment. Often the game element allows viewers to vote on who gets to leave or faces a challenge. Reality TV also has its celebrity variants, in which ordinary celebrities (or pseudo-celebrities) are placed in artificial environments. *I'm a Celebrity Get Me Out of Here!* combines the *Big Brother*-style artificial environment with challenges to eat insects and so on, voted by viewers. A series like *The Apprentice* offers ambitious would-be tycoons the opportunity to prove their worth to a Donald Trump or an Alan Sugar, with the prize being a job for the one that they choose. The weekly challenges make up the bulk of each episode, and are shot in a recognisably reality TV style. Reality TV formats are constantly moving onwards into fresh variants, combining the challenge, the artificial environment and ordinariness in various ingenious packages.

Reality TV thrives on speculation and participation. It has reinvented participatory TV and the TV event. By combining elements from the game show (the controlled challenge) and documentary (fascination with real people) it has discovered a fresh way of linking TV into the present moment of its viewers. It creates shows which excite an immediate common interest. Participants become known by their first names, as in 'Did you see what Craig did last night?' Reality TV allows unfettered opportunities for gossip and speculation by all the means that are now available: in blogs and message boards, radio phone-ins, newspapers and magazines as well as everyday face-to-face conversation. A successful reality show will have substantial daily coverage in popular newspapers and will receive distanced attention from the broadsheets as well. Its official website will keep viewers informed of the latest events, and may even charge for access to streamed live footage. In this sense, reality TV is the reality of TV: pervasively present in everyday life.

Reality TV shows encourage speculation about sincerity and the limits of permissible behaviour. These are two aspects of life that TV has been instrumental in bringing to the fore in contemporary civilisation. Sincerity is a constant issue with reality TV participants, and with it comes the issue of trust: do we trust that these people are sincere, and would we trust them? Since they have volunteered to take part in the reality TV game, they are

Q24 What is 'reality TV'?

clearly to a significant degree performing a version of themselves, or even trying to get away with a constructed persona. In game-based formats, the participants may have a substantial prize to win; in challenge-based formats they are being offered a solution to problems in their lives. In either case, it is left to viewers to judge how much they are hiding of themselves behind their performance of what they would like us to think they are. Reality TV is based on a paradox. Its situations are unreal or artificial, yet reality is what we seek from them: the reality of the individuals involved. Viewers are keenly involved in the process of decoding the 'real' people behind the performances. This process often involves a degree of sadism on the part of the viewer. We want the participants to be punished for bad or deceitful behaviour, or even just for being a type of person that we do not particularly warm to. In the morality of reality TV, deceit is the worst crime since it is a crime against the format itself. Those who enter the *Big Brother* house with a game plan, or those who treat it purely as a game show, are particularly reviled, as 'Nasty' Nick Bateman found in the very first UK series. Reality TV depends on putting the reality of ordinary people into defined artificial situations, and letting viewers discover and condone the sincere and trustworthy. Research has reported that frequent conversations about reality TV events relate directly to this issue: is it performance, or

» Q6 are they being sincere?[60]**»**

The second set of speculations around reality TV relate to the limits of acceptable behaviour. Reality TV formats tend to place participants in stressful situations, and their responses to stress can often trigger behaviour that many viewers find objectionable. As Annette Hill points out, 'Ethics are at the heart of reality programming. Rights to privacy, rights to fair treatment, good and bad moral conduct, and taste and decency are just some of the ethical issues that arise.'[61] The programmes themselves simply display behaviour. Anyone who seeks moral guidance from what happens within them is, exactly, taking them out of context. Documentary formats can provide explicit or implicit moral evaluation, but many reality TV shows

TV FAQ

do not. Apart from some challenge formats in which experts that seek to intervene and change behaviour,» reality shows provide raw material for the comments and discussions that take place around them, and these discussions are where moral and ethical questions are worked through. On message boards and blogs, people speculate freely about the possible motives of participants and what led them to behave in a particular way. They roundly condemn particular behaviours and then have to justify their views. Similar exchanges take place in everyday conversations, and are reflected in the comments of radio presenters, columnists and other media-based commentators. These reactions feed into the commentary programmes that surround the most prominent shows (e.g. *Big Brother's Little Brother*, *Big Brother's Big Mouth*, etc). The reality show may be at the core of this process, but its social importance lies in the activities it produces rather than in the series itself. As TV events rather than as TV programmes, reality TV enables public, informal discussions about the motives behind particular behaviours and the limits of acceptable behaviour.

Reality TV is part of a general social trend towards the blurring of leisure and information. It looks like entertainment, it is treated like entertainment. But it gives rise to conversations which, whilst still being compelling and enjoyable, have wider implications. Reality TV enables social talk about moral values and about how to understand human behaviour. Reality TV conversations are different from sport conversations or most other conversations around event TV. Reality TV provides neutral common ground for talking about the issues of trust and credibility of our fellow humans. Conversations about reality TV are gossip that will not get back to the subjects of that gossip, and are an opportunity for finding out what colleagues and acquaintances think about interpersonal issues without the need to confront problems together. Issues of trust and sincerity come to the fore, and then impact on other areas where these are important issues, not least the realm of politics and how politicians are regarded.»

Why are there so many challenge shows?

The great discovery of factual TV in recent years has been the challenge. Subjects that used to be treated to earnest investigative documentaries are recast as a challenge to a group of celebrities or ordinary people. Obesity? Challenge celebrities to lose weight (*Celebrity Fat Camp*). Noisy neighbours? Send them to an artificial location where they can learn to mend their ways (*World's Worst Neighbours*). Lacking social skills? Learn how to dress and behave on a date (*Would Like to Meet*). Alcohol abuse? Become a charm school graduate in just four weeks (*Ladettes to Ladies*). Lack of training and prospects? See if you can fool the experts after just a few days instruction in a specialised profession (*Faking It*). Want to make it in the music business? Try *Pop Idol*, *The X Factor* or *Fame Academy*.

The challenge suits contemporary TV because it can be stretched over a series where an investigation normally cannot. It involves a story of success or failure involving individuals with real aspirations or problems. It gets around

» Q10

the problem of making films out of people's lives» by making them willing participants in a process of change. Few challenge series have produced enduring celebrities apart from those which set out to do so, like *Pop Idol*

» Q13

and its variants.» In most formats, the challenge is met and the individuals return to their lives, enhanced. Unlike reality shows like *Big Brother*, the challenge form of the reality show involves a greater degree of control on the part of the participants. It is significant that the challenge element of *Big Brother*, a central feature of the early UK runs of the series, has become more and more atrophied. The challenges to the *Big Brother* participants tended to create forms of solidarity. These prevented the outbreaks of backstabbing and mutual loathing that have become a staple of the later series.

The challenge involves several elements. The first is that the participants recognise that they are in some way deficient. They offer themselves up for public scrutiny as people with something wrong or with unrequited desires. There is an implicit confession of inadequacy involved here, or even a recognition of social inadequacy. To acknowledge being a difficult neighbour or obese is a major part of the process of rehabilitation. The second element is the provision of instruction and support, which is sometimes the major point of a programme like *Brat Camp* or *Pop Idol*, and sometimes little more than a vague set of instructions to follow (*World's Worst Neighbours*). The series narratives show how the participants attempt to remedy their faults week by week. Several levels of commentary can be provided. The participants themselves talk to camera about their own efforts and those of others on the challenge; a voiceover narration sets the scene and measures the passing of time and milestones along the way; and there are even experts imported to provide the training or to push the challenge forward. This layering of voices provides plenty of opportunity for divergent views. Viewers can appreciate the level of self-deception among the participants, and acquire the technical vocabulary of the experts. So the third element of the challenge programme is analysis, subjecting behaviour and achievement to a consistent level of scrutiny. Then comes the fourth element: the judgement. Any challenge programme will have a concluding moment where the final assessment is made. The narrative of the series has been working up to it. Some formats take the process of judgement much further. *Ladettes to Ladies* involved expelling individuals each week; *Pop Idol* is a mass audition process with many being brutally dismissed. Some versions of the challenge process feature humiliation as a major feature.

The challenge programme shares some features of other reality TV formats, placing real people (or celebrities, who are, for these purposes, surrogate real people) into an artificial situation. They also involve, like reality TV shows, an exploration of the limits of socially acceptable behaviour. *Brat Camp* challenges out-of-control teenagers to reform themselves, sharply delineating the nature and extent of their moods and self-centredness. This is part of a general reality TV process of defining what is and is not acceptable as interpersonal behaviour in modern society. But unlike many tendencies in reality TV, the challenge formats offer more analysis. They are also explicitly concerned with transforming behaviour. They offer a form of secular salvation through their movement from confession to reforming effort and final judgement. Their overall contribution is a deeply moral one, despite (or perhaps because of) the harshness of some of the judgements on offer. The challenge series demonstrate that virtually all human beings can be improved, even though they find it difficult. They show that the initial acknowledgement of social sins is not in itself enough. It has to be matched through the series by a continual revisiting to reassess newly learned behaviours against previous habits. Self-delusion is gradually stripped away, and self-delusion is presented in many series as being the besetting sin of modern life. It provides the justification for antisocial behaviour of all kinds. The challenge format can reveal and resolve issues around self-delusion more effectively than many reality formats where challenge is less of a feature, like *Celebrity Love Island* or the latter-day *Big Brother*. Viewers enjoy the self-delusional reactions and comments in such series, but vote to reject rather than transform those whose behaviour transgresses the bounds of the acceptable.

Challenge series have a very particular place in modern factual TV, which is very different from their antecedents like the BBC's 1976 series *Living in the Past* which took a group of volunteers to live under Iron Age conditions for a year. In that series, there was a sustained attempt to stay away from personalities and to concentrate on the problems of adopting a radically different way of life.[62] Such an attitude was still evident in the BBC's *Castaway 2000* which was partially derailed by interpersonal problems. Thereafter, the challenge format began to emerge and quickly became popular as both a viewing experience and a production format. They show a process of transformation and self-improvement which can bring a quiet tear to the eyes of many viewers. This comes as the acknowledgement of the fulfilment of a narrative of real personal change, a change whose difficult stages have been the stuff of each episode of the series. Challenge series thus represent a dynamic, transformative version of the static analytic and therapeutic talk that is on offer in some daytime talk shows. As a result, some daytime shows like ITV's *Jeremy Kyle* have begun to offer a similar process of transformation, or at least confession of faults. The challenge format goes further, and offers salvation through self-improvement.

III Questions about using TV

Why is foreign TV such rubbish?

In hotel rooms and holiday resorts around the world, visitors are turning on the ubiquitous TV sets, flicking through the channels and deciding that local TV is rubbish compared to what is available back home. They usually settle for a news or sport service, or the hotel's own pay-movies. Anyone taking a little more time to browse is usually stunned by the sheer cacophony of everyone else's TV. There are all the recognisable formats like chat shows, news, stand-up and sitcom, drama, old movies, reality shows and wobbly hand-held factual footage, but everything seems at turns tedious and over-wrought. This is TV seen from the outside. What are the jokes about? Why are those people shouting at each other over something so trivial? How are these characters related, if they are? Why is the only thing worth watching an episode you actually saw two months ago? Why are there these endless debates between politicians and professors with excess facial hair? Why is the lead story on the news something of so little importance? What are the rules of this game show, and why is it on at 9pm? Why is the US series that lurks at the fringes of the schedule back home such a big hit here? Why is the dubbing so flagrantly bad? Why are the sets so cramped and flimsy? Above all, why is it so difficult to find anything interesting?

This is the experience of watching TV without the necessary points of reference. Back home, the channel brand names indicate particular kinds of TV experience, Q37, Q38 and the schedules have a known and established pattern.**》** Without these, navigation becomes extremely difficult, especially as the only familiar programme titles seem to be those of American imports. It is a chaos of material with too few established reference points. Not only is it difficult to find what you like, it is impossible to find much that is familiar beyond the formats themselves and the occasional import. The priorities are subtly different, with each nation ordering its news in a different way, putting a different emphasis on international stories, or even featuring stories that would not make it onto the national news back home. The commercials are brash, using graphics in an unfamiliar way, if they are locally produced. If not, they are exactly the same as at home, the same global brands with local voices dubbed on, which rather detracts from the exoticism of being abroad. Some of the sport is just weird, and where it is familiar, the commentaries are incomprehensible, even for someone who thinks they speak the language well. They are delivered with a speed and tone that is maddening after about five minutes. Indeed, the whole tone of TV is subtly wrong. It is either too dour or too excited, depending on whether your holiday involves snow or sun. The presenters are too distant or too intimate, they either try to ingratiate themselves, oozing smoothness, or to lecture and scold. There is too much shouting or too much muttering. Interviews are conducted in bizarre surroundings and interrupted by puzzling breaks and commentaries from elsewhere. The news shows fresh corpses at the scenes of accidents or terrorist attacks.

Chance encounters with other people's television demonstrate the extent and limits of globalisation within the medium.» It can also provide an insight into some of the difficulties that immigrants face when trying to understand our own cultures. The global brands and formats float across the surface of a TV culture which has deeper and more inscrutable roots. TV is recognisable in its outlines but different in its intimacies. There are important differences in both tone and overall visual feel which are impossible to notice about your own culture but are highly visible in other contexts. The pitch of voices, the nature of personal interactions and the tone of direct address to the audience are all things that are taken for granted within a particular culture. They are derived from, but do not directly reflect, the way that people go about their everyday business. TV in each national context has taken some elements from everyday interactions, and has added some derived from globally important TV cultures (US, UK, Brazil, etc) and has wrought a particular set of national TV rhetorics from them. Media training passes on and intensifies these skills.

» 09

Smiles and nods of the head, the use of a light touch on the arm of an interviewee, a turn up or down at the end of a sentence all have a particular televisual meaning. The meaning is derived from ordinary interactions and speech, but is altered by its use within a national TV rhetoric so that it has a specific set of connotations. This national rhetoric of TV is one of the barriers to understanding another nation's TV culture. Even for Europeans moving around Europe, TV often seems inscrutable as a result.

The second barrier is simply the everyday nature of TV, its known patterns and schedules. TV has become part of everyday life by creating and fulfilling (more or less) a number of expectations in its broad audiences. These are surprisingly deeply ingrained, leading audiences to expect not only particular kinds of programming from channels and timeslots, but also a general level of service. Some cultures expect more from TV than others, and consequently use TV more. The levels of TV viewing seem to differ radically between nations. In 2004, a UCLA survey found that Internet users in the USA watched 11.6 hours a week, whereas in Germany the same group watch 18.3 hours and Japan 20.9 hours.[63] This difference in the level of TV usage in part reflects the expectations that people have of their national TV service and how much they use other sources for audio-visual material such as DVDs, cinema visits or the Internet itself. Each national TV culture has its distinctive place in everyday life and it has established patterns of expectation amongst the general population. Without an intimate working knowledge of these patterns, it is difficult to feel at home in another nation's TV culture.

Q.27 Why do they keep breaking the rules?

In the summer of 2006, 2,635 *Big Brother* viewers complained that they had been cheated because contestants whom they had voted out were later returned to the house and the competition. They believed that the rules of the series meant that a contestant voted out was voted out permanently, and both previous series and the programme's website confirmed this. These 2,635 people complained not to the communications regulator Ofcom **»** but to ICTIS, a separate body that regulates premium-rate phone calls. They felt they had been cheated of the money they had spent on voting out their most detested contestants. ICTIS agreed and fined the premium-rate phone suppliers £15 per call, a total of around £40,000, but did not return the money paid by voters for their calls. The broadcaster Channel 4 stepped in to pay the charges saying that 'it was never our intention to mislead viewers and all profits generated from this vote were donated to charity.'[64]

Until 2006, *Big Brother* in the UK had followed a regularly stable format, despite the increasingly bizarre and disturbed nature of its contestants. In 2006, the show embarked on a new direction by introducing what seemed like increasingly desperate variations in its format. Vouchers for a place in the house were hidden in Kit Kat chocolate bars, with many lucky finders selling them immediately on e-Bay. A shadow second house was opened up midway through the series. All kinds of luxuries were provided, despite which some contestants walked out. And the contestants seemed even more bizarre than usual. One was removed almost immediately as he was suffering from a nervous breakdown. It appears that the producers knew this from 'secret diary room sessions', which would seem to contradict the idea that the *Big Brother* format offers viewers total access to the goings-on in the house. *Big Brother* 2006 was the latest in a long line of 'I don't believe they just did that' television. Both entertainment and drama formats will occasionally flout the expectancies

» Q43

TV FAQ

of viewers and sometimes even the assumptions of any sane person. Series like *Footballers' Wives* or *Prisoner: Cell Block H* deliberately offered outrageous plot developments and dialogue lines, inviting knowing and open-mouthed astonishment at the level of suspension of habitual dramatic plausibility and consistency of character behaviour and motivation. Considerable entertainment can also be created by from establishing rules and then flouting them, and a familiar rule-bound entertainment like *Big Brother* was a prime format for such treatment. It is equally possible for drama series to run against established rules. The first series of the BBC's spy drama *Spooks* starred Lisa Faulkner, an actress who had just left a high-profile role in the weekly BBC hospital soap *Holby City*. In a *coup de theatre* that was not leaked in advance, she was killed in the second episode in a particularly brutal way. This established the series as one that would break rules; however, by Series Five, the elimination of lead characters had itself become something of a *Spooks* habit.

'I don't believe they just did that' television takes three forms, all of which guarantee extensive newspaper coverage and Internet distribution of clips. It exploits the cultural visibility provided by TV by exposing the marginal or the risky to a general gaze.**»** Its first form is the deliberate flouting of genre and format rules, as in *Big Brother* 2006. The second are the rare moments when stars and celebrities behave badly on TV chat shows, like Tom Cruise jumping around on Oprah Winfrey's sofa to show how much he was in love. These are joined by the deliberate 'wind-up' series, the long line of shows that fool ordinary people from *Alan Funt's Candid Camera* from 1960, fronted in the UK by Jonathan Routh, to Dom Joly's *Trigger Happy TV* and Sasha Baron Cohen's creations Ali G and Borat. The third are those TV shows that deliberately walk on the wild side. They deliberately break taboos and set out to shock. They can take many forms, from the daytime talk of *The Jerry Springer Show* to the serious art event of Gunther von Hagen's *Autopsy* in 2002. There were the spectacles of people dared to eat worms or drink vomit in the post-pub entertainment show *The Word* or

Q27 Why do they keep breaking the rules?

the stunts of *Jackass*, or the controversial BBC dramas of the 1960s like Dennis Potter's *Brimstone and Treacle*. Some are controversial simply by the topics they choose; others, like the *Brass Eye* special on paedophilia, for the way they choose to address them.

In all cases, producers will make an appeal to a number of principles including creative freedom, the public's right to know and the need for healthy debate. Objectors ask whether it is necessary to see taboos being broken, with an emphasis on the act of seeing as more shocking than, say, a purely verbal debate. This is essentially a debate about the social role of television: whether material that offends or is liable to be imitated should be shown on such a universal generalist medium. Some material is just out for the attention it can get for itself in an increasingly crowded programme and channel market. Newspaper controversy is free publicity, and it is frequently the case that advance copies of attention-seeking shock shows will be leaked to one or two journalists. However accurately they write about the programme, it is often the case that other journalists who pick up on the story will exaggerate the problems with the programme. However, a fundamental distinction must be made between shocking for the sake of publicity and shocking in order to create a debate about social taboos. If there is a genuine desire to spark debate rather than publicity, then the channel offering shock programming will offer space for that debate, both in associated programming and its Internet presence. The presence or absence of such opportunities is what distinguishes the genuine risk from the merely risque.

Why don't you switch off and do something interesting instead?

Between 1973 and 1995, the BBC ran a children's show called *Why Don't You Just Switch Off Your Television Set And Go And Do Something Less Boring Instead?* This was a perfectly reasonable question in the 1980s, when television offered fewer channel choices and public service broadcasting still retained a residual suspicion that too much TV might be bad for you. Today's industry cannot admit this possibility. Even the BBC's own nostalgia website has been nervous about this particular programme, sneering at the quality of the series: 'Various groups of kids, e.g. The Belfast Gang, The Birmingham Gang etc would arrive every school holidays to suggest things which might be less boring than watching TV. If the programme had actually succeeded of course then it wouldn't have had an audience. ... [The title] is rather appropriate. Doing the dishes or doing your homework may have been less boring.'[65] This tone is echoed on numerous TV fan websites, which ridicule the series for being so bad that it forced people to do as its title suggested. The implication is that only really terrible TV makes you switch off.

This is TV's fantasy of itself. Since TV is multichannel and round the clock, there really should be no reason for ever turning it off. Even though multichannel TV is promoted for its convenience, providing what you want when you want it rather than when they want to show it, the industry is still nervous about the idea that people might actually want to do something else instead of watching. Watching TV is an activity that includes watching a lot of promotion for even more TV in the form of trailers and even the programmes themselves.**»** There is an overall upbeat tone of excitement at what lies just ahead. Turning away requires a certain amount of decision, insignificant for most people but difficult for a minority.**»** But everyone does turn away sooner or later, to deal with the necessities of nature or because they really do have something better

Q38

Q11

» Q39

to do. In the 'battle for eyeballs', however, this is not something that is easy for the TV industry to admit.»

TV refusniks number some two per cent of British households, according to the BBC's charter review documentation,[66] which implies something like a quarter of a million people in total. This sizeable minority feels beleaguered: 'I have lived without a television for exactly one year. Funny thing is people don't believe this. Television is now so fundamental that it's like breathing: if you stop, people want to know the reason. They suspect it's sinister.'[67] Belief in the ubiquity of TV is enshrined in the very institution itself. In collecting the licence fee which supports it, the BBC's agents refuse to believe that TV-free households exist. Warning letters are sent out to all households claiming not to have TV sets:

> 'Unfortunately, our experience over the last financial year has shown that almost half of all people who claimed not to have a television were found to be using one, and required a licence, when we checked the premises,' says a TV Licensing spokesperson. This means that when the office is notified that an address does not need a licence, officers will visit to check that this is the case. 'Once the visit is done, enquiries will stop for a number of years for those who genuinely do not require a licence.'[68]

TV refusal has many reasons. Sometimes, increasingly rarely, a particularly remote or specially located building cannot receive TV. Sometimes, people have particular audio-visual tastes that lead them to watch just DVDs of movies or Internet downloads. More frequently, people take the attitude that there is little of interest to them on TV. This is the attitude that TV watchers find the most puzzling, since it seems to them that TV touches the entire universe of interests and provides a necessary connection to the present. Certainly, the experience of reading newspapers without access to a TV must now seem strange. Not only are many stories related to TV,

TV FAQ

but major news stories (like 9/11, the Iraq War, a general election) assume that readers will have seen some TV news and are angled accordingly to provide more interpretation and less description or fact. Many TV refusniks seem disconnected from the everyday life of the rest of the population, so ubiquitous is TV in mediating and forming that everydayness. Modern society is a mediatised society, and TV has a central role in providing a general cultural visibility which is usually assumed to be universal within a particular national broadcasting culture.

This ubiquity can encourage a feeling of paranoia in those who choose to avoid TV. America's TV Turnoff Network links TV to all kinds of social ills. Even White Dot, a far more sophisticated campaign to get people to live without their TVs, tends to have a paranoid feeling about some of its pronouncements: its book *Spy TV* exposes interactive TV as an 'assault on privacy'. In the earlier *Get a Life! The Little Red Book of the White Dot*, however, the organisation provides a devastating attack on the habits of much TV programming for its narrow range of issues and repetitive plot structures. It also stages events like TV Turnoff Week, enlivened by the guerrilla use of the TV-B-Gone, a mini-remote control with just an off button that can turn off any nearby TV. Such events emphasise the unacknowledged centrality of TV in modern life, which is no bad thing in itself. TV may be everywhere but, contrary to its fantasy of itself, it is by no means everything.

Why did they axe my favourite series?

Even the longest-running TV series eventually come to an end. Their audiences, once huge, dwindle to the merely respectable. The writers and producers find it more difficult to produce fresh variations on the format, and sometimes embark on desperate attempts to introduce something fresh, which turn out to be ill-advised.[69] The stars demand more money to continue working in a 'mature' format because their desire 'to fulfil their creative potential' by 'seeking new directions' has to be bought off with increasing amounts of cash. Sometimes the audience is failing to renew itself. Between 2002 and 2006, I asked an incoming group of predominantly eighteen-year-old students whether they watched *ER* regularly. In 2002, a clear majority knew the show well. By 2006, this had dwindled to virtually none; *Desperate Housewives* had become the new 'must watch'. As a result of these pressures, the finances no longer work. Rising costs and falling audiences will lead the commissioning broadcaster (or, more rarely, the production company) to the decision to axe the show.

Nevertheless, shows like *Friends*, *Ground Force* or *Frasier* spent more than a decade at the centre of the schedules and of many people's viewing lives. The ending of a long-running series involves a weaning process through which the series becomes something to be rejected. Journalists and previewers begin to discuss how the series has gone off recently, recalling past triumphs in order to denigrate the present. Some will go so far as to question whether Monica and Chandler in *Friends*, or Niles and Daphne in *Frasier*, should have embarked on a relationship. They recall the exquisite comedy that came from Niles' excruciating infatuation with Daphne and her blissful unawareness of it. But it could equally be argued that the consummation of these relationships provided fresh impetus to the comedy enabling situations that had hitherto not existed. Somehow, these voices tend to be unheard once the 'end of series' announcement has been made. There is a subtle change in the way the last run is regarded, even if it holds on to its place in the schedules (which last runs sometimes do not). Each episode is previewed as if it were the degenerate offspring of a proud aristocratic line which has simply run out of creativity. Actors are described as coasting or 'resting on their laurels', and crucial elements of the format are suddenly seen as tired. A certain vengefulness creeps into personality journalism, with speculation about how the stars are finding it difficult to get follow-on work. *Ground Force*'s gardening star Charlie Dimmock was reported to be planning to return to work in a garden centre as her TV work had dried up. The truth of this story was limited to say the least, and the chance remarks it was based on had more to do with a family tragedy than the ending of the series.

The overall process is one that reduces the series and the enjoyment that was once and still could be gained from it. It is denigrated as 'not as good as we thought it was', becoming what some psychoanalysts calls 'a bad object'.[70] The series themselves will try to counter this wave of negative feeling by proposing a series finale cliffhanger: will *Sex and the City*'s Carrie stay with her Russian artist or get back with the recurrent Mr Big? They might produce a number of explicitly backward-looking episodes, skilfully integrating memories of the series into current business, or again the series will culminate in the production of substantial documentaries from behind the scenes that celebrate the immense creativity of the entire series team before it disperses. But these efforts have limited success as there is a larger process at work. Viewers have to be – and perhaps want to be – distanced from the series that up to that point had occupied a particular position in their viewing lives.

Even the most devoted audiences can be surprisingly pragmatic about the end of a series. They are often heavy TV viewers, and they tend to have other favourites whose developments they keep an eye on. They can shift loyalties from *Dallas* to *St Elsewhere* to *thirtysomething* to *The House of Eliott* to *ER* to *Cold Feet* to *Desperate Housewives* with relatively little sense of loss. The viewers who relate to the weaning process that subtly denigrates the series are those more numerous people who did not watch regularly at all, but had established some kind of relationship with the show. This might seem odd at first sight. But it springs from the place that television itself has in the life of its viewers» and its week-on-week currency.» The light viewer of a series gains some sense of comfort and security from the continuing presence of the show on TV, even if they do not watch very much. These series become a familiar feature in a changing world, and just the glimpse of characters in trails or the sound of the theme tune can be enough to provide reassurance that continuity exists. It is like seeing the same neighbours with whom you share the time of day but no more. But this assurance stops when the currency of the series is over, when it stops being a part of the general talk about TV and the schedules of core channels. Reruns become something else, a part of a defined past, and, oddly, TV resists nostalgia» about the past. The series has to be present in the present for this sense of companionable familiarity to operate. Once it has ceased to be part of the contemporary, it is like a neighbour who moves away and is lost from your every day existence. The weaning process is the means by which the series moves from the familiar everyday into the very different realm of memory.

» Q17
» Q33

» Q35

Why are there so many repeats?

One of the most frequent complaints from viewers is about the number of repeated programmes. And they have a point, since the mass-audience channel BBC One had 2,683 hours of repeats in 2004, making up around ten per cent of its primetime output and twenty-six per cent of its total output, whereas ITV1's output was even greater at twenty-eight per cent repeats. BBC Two repeated some 4,771 hours in the same year, thirty-four per cent of its total output, with Channel 4 at thirty-eight per cent and Five at an even greater forty-one per cent.[71] But why do repeats cause so many complaints?

At a deep level, they seems to offend against the idea that TV is always novel and always of the moment. But there are so many repeats because there is so much television. In the era of scarcity, when up to half the population could all be watching the same channel, repeats were an exception. But in the era of availability, with up to 100 channels, most people will miss most things that they might want to see. Repeat transmission is a simple device to maximise the audience for any one programme, especially when the programme cost a considerable amount to make.

Almost all everyday television programmes are virtually repeats anyway. Most programming comes in formats of multiple episodes. Drama series repeat the same characters week after week, stretching storylines over many episodes, and many take place in 'precincts' like hospitals, schools, police HQs or courts where the events involving the characters are broadly similar from week to week.**》** The humble home makeover show repeats the same plot each week with different locations and decors. A good deal of TV's domestic familiarity comes from its multiple formats that are essentially variants on the same story and characters.

This repetition of format is probably why the literal repeat of an already seen episode is so offensive to many. Audiences are attuned to the subtle variations between familiar material. Formats work by repetition with difference, by novel variation on familiar themes. To repeat actual recent material offends against this viewing habit, so mainstream broadcasters use repeats at their peril. On the mainstream channels, repeats tend to take place in radically different timeslots to the original broadcast, at the margins of the schedule. They are offered as 'another chance to see'. Repeats of factual and lifestyle programming often involve a slight re-edit and the tacking on of a cheap update on the characters, to see how their home / garden / relocation / makeover / plastic surgery has fared in the intervening months. Such repeats take place within a few months of the original broadcast. 'Classic' programmes are rerun some years after their original transmission, and situation comedies feature heavily. BBC One has been particularly fond of rerunning the sitcom *Only Fools and Horses*, particularly against a major sports or other 'must see' events on another channel, and has been rewarded with surprisingly high viewing figures.[72]

Such strategies are used by mass channels. The development of multichannel TV has transformed the pattern of repeats, producing a hierarchy of transmission for new programmes. Many series appear first on subscription-only channels; they are then rolled out on mass channels funded by commercial breaks (where they still garner the largest audiences and most publicity); and

» 037

subsequently appear on more specialised channels.**»** The major broadcasters repeat material across their groups of channels in various ways. The BBC will launch edgy youth-oriented comedy on its digital channel BBC Three, repeating it on the terrestrial BBC Two if it 'works', and perhaps even migrating it to BBC One if it looks as though it might have a broad audience appeal. This was the career of the sketch comedy *Little Britain* (developed first on radio), which became a cult in 2002 and a taste that everyone seemed to share by 2004. This is how repeating works in the multichannel era, and it has a very different function to any simple notion of 'another chance to see'. It is the way of building a reputation for a new series, particularly comedy whose characters and idiom is hard to establish with an audience. Comedy depends on being strange and oblique; television thrives on being familiar and straightforward. TV comedy has to combine the two, by becoming both strange and familiar.**»**

Once a series has become established, there are still problems with bringing it to its potential audience. *Little Britain*'s career was a cascading of acceptance by wider and wider audiences. Channel 4 collapses this roll-out into a short span, using its digital, youth-oriented E4 to provide several previews of shows like *Lost*, *ER*, *Scrubs* and *Desperate Housewives* in the week before their single transmission on the terrestrial Channel 4. This strategy ensures that the currency of a programme is stretched as much as possible. Instead of watching literally at the same time (the model of early broadcasting), a programme is available several times over a week or two. This creates a pattern like a loop or a shuttle, where there is a regular reoccurrence of the same material giving it a currency for all of its potential audience. This allows for a richer set of audience interactions than the typical exchange of the period of scarcity:[73] 'Did you see that last night?' 'No I missed it.' The characteristic exchanges of the current period run along the lines of 'Just wait till you see the next *O.C.*, you'll never believe what happens' or 'have you seen *The Mighty Boosh* yet?' Such exchanges rely on the ability to share without synchronicity. This pattern of currency will increasingly become the model for repeats as multichannel TV develops. In 2006, the BBC began to develop a model of free online delivery of programmes for seven days after their broadcast as the standard period of currency. After that period, most programmes will disappear into digital storage. However, some will be available for paid-for download. This introduces the idea of paying for repeats, neatly underlining how the cultural status of the 'repeat' is changing.

Q30 Why are there so many repeats?

How do I find my way round the repeats?

Once upon a time, you knew where you were with TV series and serials. One episode came after another in logical order. Incidents like the initial screening in 1983 by ITV of the first series of *Hill Street Blues* out of order were rare indeed. And all the bemused UK viewers were in the same boat, since they were all seeing the episodes for the first time.

How different it is now. E4 and Channel 4 show episodes from different runs of *Friends* at various times and trail a 'new' series of *The Simpsons* that has already been seen on Sky. It shows a new series of *ER* or *Six Feet Under* having already shown them on its digital-only channel E4. Where's the narrative continuity in all of that? Where once you just followed a story, now you need an archaeological sense of what you are watching: it's Frasier in his horrible long hair period; *Sex and the City* before, during or after Big; or *ER* before Julianna Margulies and George Clooney broke up. And as for *Buffy the Vampire Slayer* on BBC Two, only the real die-hards knew how to place the episodes being shown at any given time; were half the characters dead or not? If so, how definitively dead were they?

Series drama suffers from one of the great paradoxes of the multichannel era. The single drama is effectively dead, and even single filmed fiction tends to run for two hours and is often stretched over more than one evening. The aim is to hook viewers, to guarantee repeat custom, and series are the ideal means of doing that. Storylines can be developed over a run of episodes; characters become well known and complex. The downside is that casual viewers tend to be shut out as stories develop. So producers use 'last time on...' pre-credits sequences, and ingenious ideas for reintroducing their major characters in returning series. Some people have called this the 'soapisation' of TV drama. **》 Q20** But soaps are very different from series drama.**》** These are dramas that are designed to be repeated whereas soaps are not. Soaps exist in our exact present: their Christmas is our Christmas. Dramas are 'contemporary' but not co-present: Christmas in an episode of *ER* is a Christmas like ours, but not necessarily the one that we are living. Hence *ER* can be repeated and the characters can even have Christmas in July with no problems. But once we've seen a soap episode, it is used up and never repeated. Primetime drama series are designed for repetition.

Repeats not only fill hours; they produce profit on investment. In the USA, the process of syndication, the sale of programmes to be repeated on other channels or in other timeslots to their original broadcast, has been a feature of TV since the very early days. The network financing of a primetime fiction series has long provided only half the costs of actually making the series. The rest of the money and all the profits come from syndication within the US system and from sales abroad. The US level of syndicated repeats of old programming is a recent development in the UK. It means that episodes from different seasons of popular dramas and sitcoms can be seen in the same week or even in the course of the same evening on the same channel. This can be confusing for the casual viewer: the very people that long-running series need to bring in if they are to continue to prosper. It might seem as though the industry is moving in opposite directions at the same time.

The audience for TV drama series is beginning to divide into connoisseurs, regular viewers, occasional viewers and those who don't really bother that much with any of it. There is every sign of an emerging connoisseurship, a movement of fans who glean information from gossip about star's careers, and from scanning the official series websites hosted by the network, or semi-official fan sites in the USA or other territories that see episodes before the UK. Their enjoyment is not so much of what will happen

» Q17

in a series, but how it happens.**»** This is a different and more sophisticated attitude to being told a story, and then working out narrative possibilities on the basis of a little evidence. It provides the reassuring feeling of being able to predict the future. Indeed, one group of connoisseurs dispenses with the week-on-week currency of TV drama completely, and elects to watch major series on its DVD release. This reduces the time spent on the average episode of US drama from the hour slot to the actual forty minute duration of the drama without its breaks.

The chance encounter with older episodes of a series allows the busy viewer to fill in gaps, the episodes they missed the first time round, or to identify things they missed the first time round. Seeing an episode again means the deeper significance of seemingly casual exchanges or inconsequential incidents can be identified: the first time that characters met or the moment that began to change someone's mind. With multi-character series drama that is complexly plotted and expensively produced, re-seeing an episode can have this effect. For the more casual viewer it can provide a new insight into a successful series that has just begun to attract their attention, especially in the first couple of years of its life. But these multiple recalls of the past can nevertheless be disconcerting for those relatively light TV viewers who are less clear about newly emerging relationships between channels and timeslots. In its first half century as a mass medium, TV evolved gradually, so that the relative importance of channels in relation to the newness of their material was a matter of general

» 037

knowledge.» The TV industry currently can still assume that the vast majority of potential viewers possess such knowledge. However, new means of accessing TV material may erode this sense of the stratification of channels, and if this happens, then new means of navigating around the tangle of repeats will have to be developed.

Will any TV last?

08

TV belongs to the moment.**»** Much of it is used one day and discarded the next, and even its prestige and much-loved series lose their market value over time. But, after a while, the discarded items of everyday life gain in significance as they get older, and this is becoming the case with old TV programmes. For the ephemera of everyday existence, the first phase of the process of revaluation can be seen at car boot sales, where dealers seek out retro items that have become stylish again. And the apotheosis of rubbish is archaeology. Archaeologists get most of their information from 'middens', known to the rest of us as a heap of rubbish. Rubbish is vital evidence of concrete patterns of existence, providing a sense of how it felt to be alive in a particular historical moment. TV is going through the car-boot-sale phase of the process of revaluation. Like fifty-year-old food cans and packets, old TV rubbish is becoming a sought after item, valued for its retro look and the way that it makes the relatively recent past look so odd and distant. Broadcasters have now realised the value of their programmes for this kind of market, compiling programmes from extracts of thirty-year-old TV programmes so that we can marvel at the weird clothes we (or our parents) used to wear: men's kipper ties and long hair, women's garish colours and implausible designs. Alongside these come news clips of political events and comments on the naivety of programme formats and production techniques. The prevailing tone is of bemusement at how people (or we) used to live. If this is nostalgia, it is nostalgia with a contemporary twist of self-consciousness mixed with the self-congratulation.**»**

Q35

The weirdness of much old television leads some to dismiss it as rubbish, but it will provide evidence of what it felt like to be alive in the last fifty years. Indeed, it will not be the prestige programmes that are really valuable for this purpose, but the ordinary TV which is often discarded by the TV industry itself. Prestige programmes are like the piece of jewellery accidentally discarded in the archaeologist's rubbish heaps. They were made to satisfy an elite audience, often made in the image of culturally praised works of the theatre, cinema or novel. The one area of quality TV that will excite the historians of the future will be political television: documentaries, current affairs and political discussions. TV has provided the main public political arena for the last half century, and has changed politics by giving the electorate a more intimate view of politicians.» The public presentation of politics has been an important moment in the political process: indeed post-war political history can scarcely be understood without taking TV into account. Otherwise, the unique evidence offered by television will be its most ephemeral rubbish. For the historian of the last fifty years, few things will be more worthwhile as evidence than the unconsidered trifles: the variety shows and the sitcoms, the crime series and the docusoaps, the Jerry Springer freak-shows and the daytime discussions of unlikely moral dilemmas and weight loss. These will provide the evidence of what it was like to be alive in the last fifty years.

» Q7

Of course, all such evidence has to be interpreted. The archaeologist has to decide whether the presence of seafish bones in a rubbish pit far from the sea indicates a special luxury diet item or is, rather, evidence of a long-range trade in everyday foodstuffs. Equally the historian using television has to evaluate the evidence. Does a particular programme represent an ordinary or an exceptional example? Are the participants in Jerry Springer's shows intended as moral warnings or are they explicit exhibitionists who invite howls of synthetic outrage that shade into laughter? Does a particular situation comedy featuring a character who is a right-wing racist – the popular 1960s British series *Till Death Us Do Part* – indicate an acceptance of racism or a growing awareness that racism is a major social problem? These are the very real questions facing the historian using television as evidence of what life was like. They are equally things that the contemporary audience 'just knows instinctively' about the programmes, because they are living in a particular moment and are alive to the subtle connotations of everyday life.

Is any TV actually live any more?

Once all TV was live; now truly live events have a shock value because of their rarity. In the early days of TV, things going wrong was a regular occurrence, an irritant rather than a source of entertainment. The power cut that blacked out the first night of BBC Two in 1964 or the misbehaviour of animals in the *Blue Peter* studio were a couple of legendary examples of the regular lapses of live transmission. Now such events are edited out and feed a small genre of TV shows based on those outtakes; and the occasional impromptu acts of indiscrete behaviour on celebrity shows have an Internet afterlife. Live events on TV have become remarkable events, and live news events are the most remarkable of all. To have seen the events of 9/11 happen 'before our very eyes' intensified the shock of those events.**»** There seems to be a paradox here: TV technology has become far less cumbersome than it was in the 1960s, and the ability to transmit moving pictures across the globe is easy in the days of satellite, the Internet and mobile telephony. But the more mobile and instantaneous the technology has become, the less live TV we have. Live transmissions are now a tiny minority of TV output, limited to news, sport, continuity announcements, shows with a phone-in competition element or event TV like *I'm a Celebrity Get Me Out of Here!* Even in this last case, the live material will tend to be shown on a subsidiary channel like ITV2 (often with a slight time delay), or even as an Internet feed, whilst the event appears on the main ITV1 channel for a mass audience in an edited form.

The reason for the decline in live TV is clear: live material from real events is relatively tedious and almost always difficult to decipher. The live TV that dominated the early days of TV was controlled TV, transmitted from studios, planned in advance, and merely performed live. Today's live events like the news of 9/11 or sports events are heavily interpreted. The live images are immediately provided with commentary, and then are reviewed and analysed in a forensic manner.**»** They are televisualised, to

Q16

Q19, Q23

use the inspired term of John Caldwell.[74] They are brought into the TV system and are processed by it, worked over and analysed to deduce their meanings. Televisualisation has replaced the simple live images and sounds of the first years of TV with a complex processing of raw images and sounds which interrogates their meaning. It also regularises these images, editing and reframing, combining different sources, to provide a composite view which conforms to the prevailing aesthetic of TV at the time.**》** It routinely uses forms of graphics which emphasise the nature of the image as a two-dimensional artefact rather than a transfer of reality. Televisualisation transforms the live image and sound into a fully mediated representation. Yet at the same time, much TV output still aspires to many of the characteristics of liveness.

» 034

Live transmission creates a strong relationship with its audiences. It enables presenters to speak directly as though the whole apparatus of TV were simply a means of carrying on a one-sided conversation with individuals in their homes. This direct address is still a basic component of the repertoire of TV presenters, and comprises not just the adoption of a person-to-person intimacy, but also the assumption that the presenter and the audience occupy the same moment in time. Words like 'we', 'now', 'here', 'in a moment', 'today', 'this week' are routinely used to indicate this co-presence between TV show and audience. This relationship is no longer one of literal co-presence as shows are routinely taped before the transmission time and edited to provide pace and eliminate errors. Co-presence has developed into a sense of currency. TV shows may not be live, but they are current. They explicitly claim to belong to the same historical moment that their audiences are living. TV programmes are temporarily meaningful, designed to be understood by their contemporary audiences, which is why old TV looks so odd, and resists nostalgia.**》** Programmes are temporarily meaningful because they refer at will to contemporary events well known to their audiences. They themselves become the focus for a contemporary preoccupation like *Sex and the City* did around the idea

» 035

of single women dating. They convey useful information; they bring forth an intriguing character (the choleric Boyd in *Waking the Dead*; Ian MacShane's character in *Deadwood*); they grab hold of current obsessions (Bill Paterson in *Sea of Souls*) or they seize on an emerging social phenomenon like the issues of class and taste in *Footballers' Wives*. If they do this successfully, they themselves become the centre of conversation and speculation, generating press coverage and DJ chat, creating a buzz and a demand to see them. Such TV dramas also deliberately create a currency of their own: one episode follows another in a weekly pattern. Increasingly, each episode is available through several transmissions during that week, the week of its maximum currency. It is then followed by another episode with similar currency. Then the whole series enters into a cycle of decreasing currency, declining from 'the last series' to 'an old series'.» This cycle of currency allows TV drama to make references to current events in a relatively free way. Topicality is a feature of politically oriented series like *Spooks*, *The West Wing* or *Commander in Chief*. The level of contemporary reference can extend to sly in-jokes, such as Helen Mirren's line in the last episode of the occasional series *Prime Suspect*, 'Don't call me ma'am, I'm not the Queen you know', an explicit reference to her role as the Queen in the film of the same name, then showing in cinemas and destined for transmission on ITV1, the channel showing *Prime Suspect*. TV is no longer live, but it claims a currency that has developed from its live origins, and is underpinned by the fact of scheduled transmission.» The schedule, the fact that programmes have a first appearance at a defined moment in time, provides a temporal point of reference for their claim to currency. The hierarchy of channels is derived in part from their relationship to the currency of material. Major channels originate, others repeat.»

Occasional attempts are made to revive live TV forms, especially live TV drama. Live drama had a very different feel to it, not least because scenes were performed in continuity as in the theatre, rather than as dictated by production logistics, as in the cinema and filmed or

Q33 Is any TV actually live any more?

taped TV drama. This gives a theatric continuity to performances. This performance style was one component of the special aesthetic of live TV drama: it promoted an intensity of emotion and an emphasis on dialogue exchanges between couples or small groups of individuals. The physical constraints of live shooting, which meant that actors had to move quickly from one set to another, often changing their costume on the way, also gave a particular feel to live drama. There were comparatively few sets, and there was none of the elision of 'dead' time which is now routine. If a character had to move across the set before speaking their next line, we saw them do it. Speech tended to be more naturalistic, for it included the hesitations and misspoken words that pepper normal exchanges but are, again, routinely edited out in favour of a perfection of diction. Live TV drama also incorporated periods of silence, as background music and complex dubbing of sound effects and atmosphere was not possible. Some of this distinctive aesthetic can be seen in the occasional bravura live episodes of TV dramas like *ER*, *The Bill*, *Coronation Street* and *The West Wing*. However, live episodes in the USA are performed twice for different time zones, and the version subsequently distributed is edited from the 'best' takes of each.

Live TV has become televisualised, worked on by the insistent interpretation and forensic interrogation of contemporary TV. However, TV has retained and continues to rely on its principal strength, a connection with its users through the currency of much of its output.

Why does all TV look the same?

034

It's easy enough to spot a soap opera or a documentary or a talk show: they all look the same. TV production is industrial, turning out lots of essentially similar products. Just like industrial production, it is the branding that distinguishes one line of product from another, guaranteeing quality and emphasising the details that mark one essentially similar product line from another. Each talk show has its own set and graphics, but they all consist of a seated host talking with a string of celebrity guests. Each show has its gimmick (an initial conversation with a sidekick; a house band; a camera in the green room), but the format is the same: a studio set with an interviewer and guests.

Large amounts of television still come from the artificially constructed, hermetically sealed world of the studio: talk shows, game shows, soap operas, news and many situation comedies share a world of multiple video cameras that record actions on constructed sets. Since this technology operates within relatively narrow limits and is constantly innovating, at any one moment there tends to be a certain uniformity of picture – and indeed sound – quality. Video cameras have tended, for much of their history, to produce a rather bright image when compared to film used in similar situations, though extended technical developments are bringing them closer together. From this has sprung the common criticism that TV is a gaudy box of cheap jewellery. The other effect of multiple-camera studio production is that material is shot in real time, since events unfold as they are staged and visual variety is provided by cutting between camera set-ups. Live broadcasts like daytime magazine shows or news are still real-time programmes. The use of inserted material (recorded or live) provides further variety, but live daytime programming still has a distinctive pace to it, especially in markets where commercial breaks are relatively infrequent or (as with the BBC) non-existent. A BBC real time studio show like *Breakfast* (from 6.15 to 9.15

every weekday morning) involves a hectic and crowded studio floor, with guests for the following item being led silently to their places whilst the previous item is still in progress.**》** On channels with commercial breaks, the studio floor is calmer, and can be rearranged during the three or four minutes of the break. The hectic and crowded space is the control room.

》 040

Virtually all other studio material is now edited after recording. This provides a 'polish' by converting real-time activity, with all its fluffs and hesitations and boring bits, into a performance where every second is meaningful and every gesture counts. Sitcoms like *The Fresh Prince of Bel-Air* and even panel quiz shows like *Have I Got News for You* display this process for further humour, with outtake sequences at the end of shows. The editing process is both a contraction of time (eliminating unimportant moments where the action 'drags') and a dilation of time (inserting extra reaction shots or other multiple viewpoints of a significant moment so that it takes up more time on the screen than it did in reality). So editing significantly speeds up and stylises the action. This also contributes to the standardisation of the look of TV since the same kinds of so-called dead time (hesitation, extended laughter, details of entrances and exits, scene changes etc) are routinely eliminated across a wide variety of programming. The post-production of studio-made TV has also enabled the standard use of sophisticated graphics, many of which can now be used live, as they are in news bulletins. Every programme has its expensive title sequence and a distinctive set of graphics for captions identifying people, scene transitions, presentation of stills material and so on, and these are designed together with the studio sets, backgrounds and furniture to create a distinctive look which immediately brands the programme.**》** This distinctive visual regime has been called televisualisation, a particular way of constructing a composite view through television.**》**

》 023

》 033

Beyond the studio, there are still predominant looks dictated by the industrial nature of TV production. The use of standardised segments for programmes, the hour and half-hour slots, the regularity of commercial breaks, the daily, weekly and seasonal returns of episodes, all impose their constraints on the look of TV. An experiment like the film *Russian Ark*, made using video rather than film technology as a single 90-minute take, is impossible for virtually all of the world's broadcasters, as its novelty would be lost as soon as a break was inserted.**»** The world of TV production is also swept by fashion, so that an innovation is quickly imitated, becoming part of the standard repertoire of programme looks. So the use of lightweight, single-person-operated video equipment in documentaries soon yielded a standard form, the conversational interview conducted from behind the camera whilst the interviewee is doing something else, often driving a car. Similarly, video diaries, originally an innovation of the BBC Community Unit, soon became a common part of the repertoire for travel shows, consumer shows and celebrity programming.

Drama series deliberately create a branded look to mark them out from all others. For *ER*, it is the swift-moving Steadicam shots, weaving in and out of action that is staged in extreme depth on an elaborate set. For *Without a Trace*, it is the flashbacks drained of colour that propose possible explanations for the events under investigation. For *Ally McBeal*, it was the sudden irruption of fantasy, often with music and even with animated figures, into the life of the law firm in which she worked. For a series like *Heartbeat*, it is a deliberately old-fashioned pace in accord with its period setting in the rural Britain of the 1960s.[75] The trademark look of each drama is often created by exaggerating or going against one single aspect of the current norms of visual style for drama. *ER* moves the camera rather than cutting; *Without a Trace* proposes flashbacks that are mere speculation rather than, as is normal, a revelation of truth;**»** *Ally McBeal* allows subjective fantasies to invade the objective action etc. A series like *NYPD Blue* borrowed a visual style from on-the-spot news reporting and elaborated it by inserting random cuts to the reframed shot from the same point of view. In each case, the achievement of a trademark look was a tremendous investment of time and

Q38

Q19

Q34 Why does all TV look the same?

invention. Yet in all other respects these dramas still look like all others. Their stars have the same make-up and naturalistic acting style, the sets and locations conform to current norms, and their budgets, though generous, are a fraction of those commanded by Hollywood film-makers. On lower budgets, a distinctive look for a series is less easy to obtain. The look of studio-made multi-camera soap operas is virtually indistinguishable. In the UK, primetime soaps can command rather greater resources, which are chiefly invested in highly realistic and robust standing sets.

The extent to which TV has a particular standard set of looks becomes clear when older material is repeated. The pace is different, particularly with studio material made up to the mid 1970s when post-production editing of video was less established and much more expensive. The actions take place much more in real time, with a significant number of mistakes, hesitations and fluffed lines.**»** At the time of their original broadcast, these programmes conformed to the norms of TV production: the pace of the action, the over-brightness of the image, the pitch of the performances, were all perfectly normal. This will be the case with current TV when seen again in twenty-five years. We watch TV so routinely that we become used to the current general look, and quickly appreciate the trademark variations that are made by prestige series. These will become less obvious as the overall look of TV evolves as a result of both technological innovations like widescreen and high definition, and the constant search for an innovative and competitive edge.

» 035

Why does old TV look so weird?

Most TV programmes do not age gracefully, as many films do. Many old films can be re-experienced with a warm glow of nostalgia after twenty years or more. Sitcoms and some drama (especially those series that were set in the past to begin with) can evoke such feelings, but the vast majority of programmes do not. Old episodes of soaps are at best the specialist pleasure of the devoted fan. Old game shows, old variety or talk shows, old documentaries are more often regarded as 'cringeworthy'. They provoke feelings of embarrassment and discomfort. Even children's TV from our youths tends to be re-watched more with disbelief and mockery than recalling the emotional experiences that that they once provided.

On the face of it, this is odd. These programmes were so much a part of the texture of everyday life that they should surely be rich with nostalgia. Instead they are full of irritating details. There are the strange hairstyles and fashions which people cannot now believe seemed normal or even the height of fashion. The actors and presenters seem eager and naive compared to the graver and more complex and even careworn maturity that they now enjoy. Somehow their voices are pitched higher and their movements seem gauche. Their accents are subtly less demotic, closer to what, after all, is called BBC English or received pronunciation. The sets seem preposterous, too flimsy and extravagant at the same time, with garish colours. In the dramas set in contemporary times, the details do not seem quite right. The music seems to be more modern or a lot older, but certainly not of that precise period. The cars seem to come from a slightly later era than the clothes; there are items of technology that surely didn't exist at that time; monetary values are just incomprehensible. Did anything ever cost 'half a crown'?[76] The past on its TV programmes is just not how we remember it to have been.

This strange dislocation between our personal memories (or preconceptions) and what we are seeing causes feelings of discomfort and embarrassment rather than nostalgia. For these programmes are small fragments of very particular pasts. Nostalgia relies on a more generalised sense of the past. Nostalgia after all is not something that lies in wait within a piece of music or a film. It is something that we experience in relation to the music or film; nostalgia comes from the viewer or listener and not from the text. Nostalgia is the experience of the past as an individual imagines or wants it to have been, which is by no means necessarily what it actually was. Some critics go so far as to say that nostalgia comes from what the present is seen to be lacking, that people will construct an idealised past which fulfils everything that the present does not. 'The simple, pure, ordered, easy, beautiful, or harmonious past is constructed (and then experienced emotionally) in conjunction with the present – which, in turn, is constructed as complicated, contaminated, anarchic, difficult, ugly, and confrontational.'[77] This may well be one reason why many TV programmes resist nostalgia. They are too much of their time, too literally of the moment, to be easily assimilated into a view which seeks to idealise the past in relation to a difficult present.

Old television material can even seem vaguely repellent. How on earth did we ever think this was modern and contemporary when now it seems so arbitrary and alien? Why were we so taken in by this stuff at the time, when our TV programmes now seem so much better? Current TV programmes are classier and 'better produced', whereas old TV is the domain of clunky sets, slow action, mannered acting, cheesy costumes and gestures. Present-day TV seems better rather than worse in the main, even though there are inevitably some kinds of programmes that we miss. However, few would want to revive variety shows like *The Black and White Minstrel Show*, a standard feature of BBC Saturday nights for many years; nor would they want to being back the empty glamour of *The Persuaders!* or the plots of *The Saint*, however good or handsome an actor Roger Moore might have been in both series. TV's past is too profoundly ambiguous to be easily idealised in relation to the present.

Yet there seems to be more involved in nostalgia than an idealisation of the past. The feelings that nostalgia can provoke are strong, seemingly triggered by little details that seem to bring back whole experiences and whole important moments in time. The reason for the emotion might be a dissatisfaction with the present or a longing for what is now lost. Such feelings of nostalgia can be provoked by details and not by the whole film or programme. But this rarely happens with TV, though it can often be the case with film. The reason lies in the references that are made to everyday life and common phenomena: references to what it costs to buy something, to well-known people or events, to things that most people take for granted. Such cultural references in films tend to be slightly more generalised than those on TV since films are made for a more diverse and global audience. The little local details are smoothed out in anticipation of a wider audience: more distant both in geography and in time from the moment of original production. British TV will be able to refer quite unselfconsciously to well-known people or events from football or cricket. The producers of a film will work hard to insert explanatory material so the reference, or the meaning of the reference, is entirely clear to anyone who has never heard of the particular person, or even is unaware of the rules of cricket, incredible though that may seem.[78] Film ensures clarity and in doing so smoothes out the incidental detail and the things of the moment. This is often the result of progressive drafts of script and long discussions of questions of design. A TV show destined for a relatively short life in the public eye need not go to such lengths. The result is that much TV is suffused by things of the moment from which it sprang, and for which it was made.

This level of the incidental and accidental, the things of the moment, seems to be the real block to nostalgia. There is so much of the intimate texture of the past in old TV programmes that it is often rather disconcerting. This is feeling that the bits do not quite fit together, that clothes, music and gesture do not gel into a remembered historical moment, or rather that, if they do, they are startling rather

Q35 Why does old TV look so weird?

than comfortable. For what comes in an old TV programme is a fragment of a moment rather than a more considered sampling as would be found in a film. This sense of the moment runs against the mechanisms of remembering, which also tend to generalise. Everyday events are run together into the memory, so that we say 'we used to do this' to cover a whole set of specific things. Memories of everyday things are also generalised, becoming a category that belongs to a period, as in 'the kind of clothes we used to wear back then'. These general categories are then further augmented by the kind of associations that they attract, the kinds of associations that can well lead to more general nostalgic recall.

This generalising aspect of memory for everyday things comes up against the very specific and concrete moment that is embodied in many old TV programmes. It brings about a feeling that something is not being quite right in the programme; that it is not quite as we recall the past. Generalised memories indeed do not fit together very well, for they generalise rather different time frames: the memory of the everyday is not of whole moments but of trends and of bits, each with their own time frame. The absolute momentariness of much past TV runs against this. It is not so much from the past as in the past, not so much of the moment as still in the moment. As old TV is so much of the past, much of it resists nostalgia. The exception is those more timeless genres, like sitcom, where nothing much has changed since the early days of

» Q18

TV.» The resistance of much old TV to the workings of nostalgia may have an unexpected advantage, however. It can give an unexpectedly vivid insight into what it felt like to be alive in a particular moment, which can act as a counterbalance to both hindsight and to inaccurate

» Q32

historical generalisations.»

Questions about technology and the TV industry

How does this stuff get made anyway?

» Q22

TV production is much more of a factory process than feature-film production. A single programme is a rarity, as most ideas are developed into a number of episodes.» Each episode will be slightly different, however. A show like Channel 4's *Countdown* may have run for more than 5,000 editions, but the contestants are different in each and the show evolves slowly over time. So the process is not that of an assembly line so much as a routinised form of work, in which most creative decisions are already taken, and everyone involved knows what is expected of them. TV production is routinised at all levels, bringing a degree of certainty to the production process, which is fraught with risk and creative wastage.

Series are produced within a framework of common understandings. Each genre has its production habits, so it is possible to assemble a team with a common sense of purpose, and the producers of a groundbreaking production can explain how it will be distinctive to those commissioning. When the producers of *The Royle Family* proposed a sitcom that would be shot in a conventional living-room set, but without studio audience and with a single camera, it was clear to the BBC that a considerable level of creative risk was involved. The risks were mitigated by the established talent involved, including Ricky Tomlinson and Sue Johnston, who had, from 1982, spent five years playing husband and wife in the Channel 4 soap *Brookside*.

The level of standardisation within TV is reflected in the 'guide prices' that are issued by broadcasters when they put a slot or format out to tender in the production community. The price is only a starting point for negotiation on the chosen project, but to tell a producer that a drama will cost 'x' per episode rather than '2x' is to send powerful messages about the expected nature of the product. Running time and proposed schedule slot are the other major methods of establishing standardisation. A skilled producer can 'read' the probable level of the production budget just by looking at a TV programme produced in their own market.[79]

Production standardisation is different in each national production market.» It underpins the organisation of production, enabling workers within the production community to move easily between projects for all the channels within that market. It enables crews to have a common understanding about the nature of the project they are working on; it enables broadcasters and producers to have meaningful conversations about creative ideas. Finally, it enables production work to become more collectivised, leading to developments such as team scriptwriting.» To become a key production worker within a particular market, it is essential to acquire a sense of its underlying culture of standardisation. However, standardisation is by no means total: each programme in a series may be similar, but each has to have new elements. TV production is repetition with variation.»

One of the principal sources of variation within TV formats is the assumption that they will be current, addressing the present moment.» TV quiz shows may be recorded in batches of four or more a day, but even these intensive production weeks are spaced out through the year. This may seem inefficient, but changes in the wider world may suddenly render questions inappropriate, or answers incorrect; some personal catastrophe may overtake one of the cast (either presenters or contestants) between the recording and transmission. So a quiz show featuring someone convicted for a major crime since it was recorded would not be transmitted. TV has to be up-to-the-minute, so TV production is undertaken on a just-in-time basis rather than in huge batches, which would possibly be more efficient for many long-running series.

The framework of common understandings about the nature of programmes is necessary because everything else is highly uncertain. The financing and commissioning of TV series of any ambition is becoming ever more complex. The American system of deficit financing or co-producing major series is becoming more widespread in Europe. The principle is simple enough: with the development of

Q36 How does this stuff get made anyway?

multiple opportunities for buying and selling programmes to different kinds of channel across the globe, the channel that originally commissions a series need not necessarily pay for the whole production budget. There are other ways of financing based on the expectation of future sales both in the home market (called 'syndication' in the US) and in export markets. Further income might be expected from spin-offs from the series: the sale of the format abroad; the sale of associated products and services (from T-shirts to advice services); and from premium-rate phone calls for programmes involving viewer participation. So a variety of finance packages can be developed based on this investment potential.

» 037 The channel of first broadcast has crucial power in this relationship.» The channels of first broadcast are usually the traditional terrestrial broadcasters and have had long traditions in producing their own programming. When such channels produce their own programming, they will control all the subsequent sales and income, but almost all now commission at least some of their programming from independent production companies. Channels that commission all their output from independent suppliers are still a rarity despite the innovative creation of Channel 4 in 1982. As the nature of the TV market changes, the traditional channels are increasingly aware that their future lies in exploiting their known editorial identities as trusted suppliers of particular kinds of programming, so they increasingly try to control as many aspects of their programming as possible.

However, large corporations with many varied responsibilities and interests are not necessarily the best places for creative activity, even within a relatively routinised industry like TV. It is still remarkably difficult to imagine new formats and to get them to work, or to create viable new fiction series that will enthuse choosy audiences. A focused production company often provides a better creative environment, and this is the reason for the rise of independent production. Independent production companies are by no means necessarily small enterprises. They can have hundreds of staff and be involved in many different projects. Their single focus on creativity is their single advantage in the market, but they still need a broadcast channel to reach a substantial audience with their ideas.

The channel of first broadcast will have a strong brand and will regard any series that it commissions from an independent supplier as a contribution to that overall identity. The channel's editorial staff will have substantial input into the creation of the series, from the initial idea to detailed scripts, from casting to the overall visual style. The channel will pay for such involvement as it is a process of partnership: it is cheaper to buy completed programmes than to commission them, but broadcasters need to put their distinctive editorial stamp on their keynote output every day of the week. The initial broadcaster will make a substantial investment in any new series, and often has the bargaining power to obtain a substantial share of future income as well. The major channels still control access to the market for independent producers. Without an airing on a major channel, almost all output is still condemned to the relative obscurity of niche-channel viewing or new forms of distribution. Despite a quarter of a century of multichannel TV in the US, this is still largely the case.

Q43 Various forms of regulation exist to make this market work in a more equitable way.**»** In the UK, a legal minimum of independent production of twenty-five per cent of their new output has been imposed on the major broadcasters since 1991, and this has more recently been coupled with further regulations to prevent them 'buying out' all the rights to further sales from the independent producers. From 1970, the US regulatory body the FCC maintained a regulation preventing the networks from participating in income from syndication. This forced the development of a system of deficit financing which meant that the producers of major drama series turned to distribution companies to raise around half their budgets. This built on the established system in the movie industry. By 1995 the 'fin-syn rules', as they were called, were finally abandoned, allowing the networks to acquire many if not all the rights in shows commissioned from third parties

Q36 How does this stuff get made anyway?

and thus to secure their ongoing brand interest in those series.

By that stage, the production sector had developed large-scale enterprises of its own: producer-owned networks like News International's Fox TV and near-networks like HBO had emerged in specific areas. The involvement of a major channel does not guarantee success, and the relationship between creators and broadcasters is often strained. The US system works on the expectation that several major series will be cancelled early into their first season, depending on 'the sweeps', an in-depth audience survey carried out five or six weeks into the new broadcast season.**》** Sometimes, as was the case with *Hill Street Blues*,**》** a broadcaster, in this case ABC, will decide to maintain a series despite low ratings because it can see particular kinds of potential. Cancelled series may already have been sold to overseas broadcasters who will have planned them into their following season's schedules, and they have to rethink their plans.

》 Q39
》 Q20

TV production is a production-line process, making long runs of similar programmes, each of which differs from all others. It involves a considerable degree of routinised work from skilled staff,**》** often under the pressure of an impending deadline to ensure the currency of the production. The activity of creation is dispersed across different groups, and much of it takes place at some distance from the actual moment of shooting.**》** The financing of production is becoming increasingly complex as TV diversifies.

》 how to
get job

》 precinct

What is a channel?

Q38

A channel brings a stream of programmes to viewers. Analogue terrestrial channels each occupy a particular waveband and send signals across it which are watched (or recorded) at home by their viewers in real time. Each channel schedules its programmes for the moments of the day which it believes will be most convenient and desirable for its potential viewers.**»** A channel is therefore more than a technical structure. It creates an identity through the kinds of programmes it provides and the way it places them in relation to each other. It uses the particular tones of voice of its presenters and announcers to create the idea of a particular group of people, or kind of person, who give life to the channel. It uses particular kinds of graphics to express its identity.

In the UK, BBC Three and E4, both aimed at a youth market, used quite similar graphic strategies during 2005/2006. Both had quirky animated characters: E4's were line drawn and BBC Three's were 3D models. A channel also relates one programme to another by placing trailers for its future transmissions. In the USA, with a more dispersed geographical market spread over several time zones, national channels are referred to as 'networks' because they supply blocks of programming to local broadcasters. The network affiliation of a local station is the core of its identity, and in this sense the US networks are channels.

A channel is a complex brand. So complex is it that even marketers find it hard to sum up in words, yet every viewer has a sense that each of the channels they use has a distinct identity. There are programmes that you would expect to find on Channel 4, and others that you would on BBC One: *Big Brother* on Channel 4 and David Attenborough presenting *Planet Earth* on BBC One, for instance; *Hollyoaks* or *Grand Designs* on Channel 4 and *EastEnders* and *The Big Day* on BBC One. There is an overall Channel 4 attitude (naughty but well-intentioned and slightly low-budget) and a BBC One attitude (inclusive and responsible, prosperous and competent). Each channel has a distinctive attitude to imported US programming,» with Channel 4 using shows like *Desperate Housewives* as a major feature of their schedule and BBC One being far more sparing.

Channels are more complex and enduring brands than programmes. They offer an editorial approach to what they choose to include in their broadcast flows, which is expressed through their schedules. The clear brand identities of particular programme series contribute to the much larger overall feel of a channel. Established programmes may be moved from one channel to another, but tend to be subtly transformed in the process, as was *24* in its move from BBC Two to Sky, or *Lost* from Channel 4 to Sky. In both cases, there was a considerable loss in audience as the change tainted the programme brand in the UK market. Expectation-based viewing habits were disrupted, and there may have been a feeling that the BBC and Channel 4 had 'let the series go' because they felt they were going downhill, even though the fundamental reason was simply that they had been outbid for the rights.

Channels are increasingly aware of their brand identities as they evolve to deal with the new TV environment. Channels are no longer single; they exist in families with complementary brands: the single generalist ITV channel has become ITV1; ITV2 carries programmes that continue or relate to ITV1; ITV3 repeats classic UK drama originally shown on ITV1; and ITV4 has a varied schedule of repeated imports. They have a common graphic style. Each channel in the brand family cross-promotes their offerings. Programmes are scheduled in a complementary rather than competing way. Each channel itself is no longer a single stream of scheduled content. The scheduled channel sits at the centre of a multi-layered web of programme activities, giving it its overall identity and coherence. The channel brand can attract material made by its viewers, comments and debate on its website as well as downloads of already-aired episodes and premium paid-for viewings of those yet to air on the broadcast channel.

Leslie Moonves, the CBS boss, argues that the traditional US networks have been able to use their clear brand identities and strength in the TV market to guide viewers to programmes. As he puts it, only half in jest:

> The most loyal viewer of a network TV show ... only watches two out of four episodes. Unfortunately for us in the TV business, people occasionally have a life. They like to go out to dinner every once in a while and miss television. They shouldn't. We dissuade them from doing that. In the new digital age ... you can now come home after dinner and download the episodes you missed. Digital is only going to expand our audience.[80]

Moonves' strategy is to use the strength of the channel's identity to enhance and give shape to the identity and appeal of new programmes. Channels both create new programmes (like CBS's *CSI* series) and bring together programmes from elsewhere into a coherent space which bestows on them the particular identity of the channel. They offer an editorial approach to all that they carry. In the fashionable phrase, channels are aggregators of programme content. A channel is a particular kind of trade mark which guarantees a level of quality to all that it encompasses.

This means that the strong channel identities will continue to play a major role in any future TV market. But will TV channels in a scheduled form continue to exist? The structured flow of programmes streamed to potential audiences is often seen as being under threat. In fact, the current market is divided between three kinds of channel. The first is the most traditional: the old broadcasters like the US networks, the BBC, ITV, Channel 4 and Five, France's TF1 and so on. They carry a mixed schedule addressed to a wide coalition of interests and social groups. Most have spin-off channels which are more targeted to particular groups. These have a subsidiary identity, like Five US, More 4, BBC Four, and have a tight brand relation with the generalist channel. A second model is the channel (or

Q37 What is a channel?

family of channels) with a highly distinctive almost genre-based identity, like Cartoon Network, HBO, Discovery, UKTV Gold – 'niche channels' in the jargon, which carry a high level of syndicated programming that originally appeared on or was created by the major networks under the banner of their strong brands.**»** The third is the service model. New broadcasters like Sky whose identity relies on an image of plenitude: it is a service offering lots of material rather than a single channel. Indeed, Sky One struggles to define its identity against the traditional broadcast channels.

» Q30

Curiously, it is the niche channels that seem most under threat in the emerging new order of TV. Traditional channels offer an editorial approach to a wide range of programming, but the niche channels offer just the same kind of programmes, often repeated in blocks through the day. This form of delivery is a clear compromise with available technologies. They are new-screen brands aching to escape from the old-screen technology of the broadcast stream. Most niche channels would easily transform into a download-on-demand model or the model of automatic delivery to a storage device like a PVR 'in case you want to watch'. A channel like HBO might well be an exception to this as it has more in common with traditional broadcasters. The traditional broadcast channels offer something more than niche channels: they offer a link between different kinds of content, and a link with the time of day in which they are offered. They offer a service rather than a random assemblage of material.**»** And they offer a distinct viewing experience of editorialised broadcast streams that is different from new-screen forms of delivery.

» Q42

What is a schedule?

A major TV channel presents a stream of programmes through the day and most, if not all, of the night. The schedule is the term for the way these programmes are arranged: the day and time of day on which they will be shown, what they will follow and precede, how long they will last. Schedules carve the twenty-four hours into half-hour and hour-long slots, each of which will include programmes, advertising, trailers and announcements. A typical 30-minute slot will contain between twenty and twenty-six minutes of programme, depending on the length and frequency of advertisement breaks. This provides a powerful sense of regularity and predictability to the entire channel-based TV experience.

Schedules are particularly important for those channels, like the major terrestrial channels, that provide a wide variety of programming. Their schedules provide the channel's standard pattern, which is a key part of its known identity.**»** Habitual TV viewers have a working knowledge of where to find their favourite programmes and the general pattern of what that channel is likely to be offering, particularly in the evening primetime. There are long-term fixed points in every channel's schedules, like soap episodes at 7pm or 7.30pm on weekdays, and news bulletins at 6pm and 10pm. There are others slots that tend to contain the same kind of programming (like major drama at 9pm on Mondays), building expectancies among the audience. The surrounding slots will be far more fluid in what they contain, providing considerable flexibility for schedulers to place new programming where they hope it will receive maximum attention. They also enable schedulers to experiment with grouping programmes into strands, particularly comedy, to create an overall feel for a particular evening of the week.

Schedules define programmes and provide a convenient navigational shortcut for viewers. They work by matching programmes to times of the day, associating them with particular zones: late-night, daytime, or peak-time before

037

» 043

or after the watershed (the term for the 9pm moment when regulators» allow more adult-oriented content). Schedules associate programmes with the potential audiences and what they are likely to be doing at the time. So, in the UK, the early evening will contain more soaps and magazine or lifestyle programmes which can be watched while there is a lot of coming and going in most households, like preparation and consumption of meals, getting ready to go out, phone calls and conversations. The later evening, from 9 o'clock onwards, tends to be the period for more sustained watching, of fiction and more analytic documentary material. Daytime has a different character. There is more stripping of weekday schedules; that is putting the same programme on in the same slot every day. Audiences are much smaller in number than evening primetime. Students, the retired, carers, night-workers and the unemployed usually predominate. Such disparate audience groups tend to be drawn together by a mixture of talk shows that centre on emotions, repeats of yesterday's soaps and more prolix lifestyle and challenge shows like *Flog It* (buying and selling small antiques) or game shows like *Supermarket Sweep* (competitive grabbing from supermarket shelves).

Successful daytime shows can be moved to evening slots, thereby gaining in audience size, press attention and general esteem. This was the case with both *The Weakest Link*, presented by Anne Robinson, and *Deal or No Deal*, presented by Noel Edmonds, both of which became major successes and somehow more prestigious when moved from daytime to evening slots. The slot in which a programme is scheduled says much about it, since slots imply larger or smaller levels of budget and esteem. The schedule also links series into a particular time of day or week, endowing them with a regular connection with their audiences, enabling them to insinuate themselves into the

» 02

everyday lives of their viewers.»

This produces the deep sense that the activity of television broadcasting itself proceeds in the present moment and addresses the present moment. The regular patterns of the schedule give much television an intimate feeling of contact with its audiences. So the pattern of a channel's schedule extends beyond the division of the day to differentiate parts of the week and even the seasons. In the UK, the distinction between weekday and weekend is marked by the scheduling of soaps during weekday evenings; blocks of comedy programmes on a Friday evening; middlebrow drama on a Sunday evening; and family drama and variety shows like *Ant and Dec's Saturday Night Takeaway* on Saturday. These keynote programmes respond to the character of those days in many people's lives. Schedules also change according to seasons, offering a range of predetermined and unanticipated events ranging from sport and TV-generated events like *I'm a Celebrity Get me Out of Here!* to news-driven material and special schedules for the Christmas and New Year season and other major holidays.

Scheduling is a competitive process, and audience statistics are central to it.❯❯ Schedulers examine the reported audience composition of their programmes in particular slots. They try to work out what the movements of audiences might be, why particular kinds of people switched towards or away from their offerings at a particular time. They compare the composition of their audiences with those of the other channels to see whether there are potential viewers who seem to be being offered too little or too much. Programmes are designed or redesigned to increase their appeal to under-provisioned groups. Programmes that are competing for the same over-provisioned groups can be moved to slots where they have a better chance of reaching those audiences. Alternatively, they can be cancelled entirely. The scheduling order of programmes provides a key promotional opportunity, as there is an 'audience inheritance' from one show to another. This is exploited by the use of trailers during advert breaks, and by announcements over end credits. Significant promotional advantages can be gained for new programmes by placing them after popular programmes, or even between them, a traditional practice known as 'hammocking'.

The schedule underpins the familiarity and comfort of TV as a medium. It gives it patterns which respond to the

Q39

Q.38 What is a schedule?

changing times of day, week and season, the special days and the ordinary ones. A clear schedule can provide a channel with a distinctive identity, and it builds audience expectations and valuations of particular programmes. It is also the focus of much of the competition for audiences between channels. The nature of one channel's schedule and its relationship with those of other channels determines decisions about what programmes are or are not commissioned. The schedule of a particular channel, therefore, is key in determining its distinctive character. The editorial processes of a channel, which give it a distinctive identity, are expressed through and structured by its schedule. One channel may have a Thursday comedy strand; another will concentrate on gardening programmes on a Friday or sport on a Sunday afternoon (BBC Two). Another will strip imported American drama or a cinema film at 9pm for five nights a week, and run arts programming in the early evening when other channels have news or programmes oriented towards young people (Five). Through such scheduling strategies, the channel clearly expresses its identity.

The diversification of audiences and channels has produced more finely differentiated editorial approaches in channel scheduling. This in turn has had an impact on the kinds of programmes that are commissioned and produced. Dating programmes on UK TV provide a vivid example. For many years, there was really only one dating show on British television. ITV had a hugely successful dating programme as the keystone of its early Saturday evening schedule: *Blind Date*, hosted by Cilla Black. The format was simple. Three male candidates were interviewed by Cilla, and then chosen from behind a screen by a female who asked them three questions. This formula was then reversed, with one male choosing from three females. Each resulting couple was sent on a week's holiday 'to see how they got on', and reported their experiences in the following Saturday's programme. Cilla's maternal but flirtatious and suggestive performance as presenter held it all together. After eighteen years, Cilla used the 4 January 2003 live edition to announce on air that she was quitting as presenter. Her employers knew nothing in advance. One of Britain's enduringly popular presenters ensured that her audience, rather than her bosses, would know first. Her decision was a wise one, wiser than the ITV schedulers who had kept the show on, perhaps. *Blind Date*, which once attracted an audience of seventeen million, had declined to around four million. Once it was an essential feature of the early Saturday evening, offering a warm-up to the weekend party scene for teens, an anticipation of future dating for pre-teens and a discussion opportunity for parents. *Blind Date* was the dating show for all the family, and indeed the only regular dating show on air.

The family nature of the programme was its undoing. The family-together viewing of early Saturday evening was a thing of the past by the end of the last millennium. Dating shows themselves had proliferated across the schedules of other channels, and there was even an entire Dating Channel (basically a noticeboard operation) on Sky and cable. Dating had moved out of family entertainment into a number of different niches, all of which concentrated on the young and the heterosexual, and was beginning to acquire some of the habits of reality TV.**»** Even Cilla had for some time recruited exclusively from the most colourful elements to be found in university bars,[81] but a family show at 7pm could do little with them. The core of the show was the innuendo that Cilla, every contestant's auntie, could get away with, rather than the antics of contestants or the post-date insult ceremonies. Late-night factual programmes like *Ibiza Uncovered* had already gone beyond this by showing what did happen on such dates. They explored sexual habits, the mysteries of attraction, and their lack of fit with the everyday business of existence, plus plenty of naked flesh.

The proliferation of dating shows continued, with late-night dating shows like Five's *The Honey Trap* featuring three models who lured males back to their Ibiza villa and challenged them with various degrading tasks. The intensification of the humiliation element in dating spread to primetime, especially when it involved humiliation across the generations within a family. MTV's *Date My*

» Q24

Q38 What is a schedule?

Mom took one element of *Blind Date*'s format – the fact that the suitor does not see their date until the choice is made – and developed it: the man has to date the mother instead and choose a daughter on the basis of the possible mother-in-law and her account of her daughter. The Dutch format, *Who Wants to Marry My Son*, worked the other way, by involving a mother in the choice of a potential bride for her stay-at-home son. Fox's series *Joe Millionaire* took a handsome, if self-obsessed, builder and made twenty women compete for his affections. They all thought he was a millionaire, though, and the show's appeal lay in the fact that the audience knew he was nothing of the kind. ITV's attempt at the same format, *Mr Right*, flopped because it did not have that game show humiliation element.

The BBC had similar problems. It bought the format of NBC's *Meet the Folks*. This makes the datees' family decide which suitor will go on a luxury cruise with their offspring, producing plenty of embarrassing situations and revelations. The series was clearly an attempt to appeal to the audience that Cilla had just abandoned and was shown around 6pm on Saturdays. It was intended to provide a more public-service» twist to humiliation by showing inter-generational differences of opinion. *Meet the Folks* did not work. Five programmes of the twelve originally made were shown on Saturdays in June and July 2003. The other seven were relegated to a late-night slot (11.30pm) on Fridays from October. This rescheduling turned a family show into post-pub amusement, and it is possible that some re-editing took place to reflect this.

The new phenomenon of speed dating also produced formats. ITV experimented with two: *Love Match*, where contestants had to spot the one speed dater who fancied them from three who were lying; and *Cupid*, where the woman whittled down speed daters to a shortlist whose subsequent attempts to seduce her were judged by a panel of her friends presided over by *Pop Idol*'s Mr Nasty, Simon Cowell. Dating shows had become a genre, producing different levels of sexual explicitness and mockery of participants depending on their place in the schedule of the particular channels that were offering them. *Blind*

TV FAQ

Date's Saturday evening monopoly, the result of relatively constrained scheduling opportunities, gave way to a range of approaches, each of which was defined by its place within the schedule of the particular channel commissioning the series.

Scheduling is an editorial process. It is now far more than simply placing programmes in an order and at times that might attract a large audience. The schedule now determines what kinds of programmes are commissioned and made. It provides familiar patterns to particular channels and groups of channels. The schedule expresses the distinct identity of a channel, and so is key to the future market importance of channel-based broadcasting.

Does TV exist to sell audiences to advertisers?

» Q42

For almost all its existence, TV has understood its audience in terms derived from advertising. In the USA, television was from the start a medium that relied on advertising. When commercial TV arrived in other countries, advertising-oriented audience surveys soon followed, whether this was the Great Britain of 1955 or the Norway of 1992.» The UK started with a plethora of different ways of measuring the audience, but this was replaced in 1964 by general agreement between the BBC, ITV and the advertisers' association, with one set of figures paid for by all. This arrangement evolved into the British Audience Research Bureau (BARB) in 1981. Since the 1960s this joint agreement has provided a commonly accepted measure of the numbers and types of people watching TV. The kind of data collected is skewed towards an advertiser's view of the audience. It asks what kind of people are watching a programme: how old they are, what social class they belong to, whether they are male or female, what region they live in.

This assemblage of demographic information fits well with the requirements of mainstream marketing and its understandings of how to target particular sections of the community. For instance, BARB figures will tell, with a reasonable degree of accuracy, how many women over sixty and children under ten of social class DE were watching Channel 4's *Countdown* in the North East of England on a particular day. It will not, however, give any information on how much they enjoyed it, whether they were habitual or occasional viewers, what else they were doing at the time or immediately before and afterwards, and other information that would be useful to programme-makers, sociologists and the just plain nosey. But they do provide ratings, and ratings define audiences and the success of programmes. BARB is, cumulatively, the only real information that exists about the everyday habits of the TV audience.

The system is an expensive one to run, costing over £12 million a year. It meters all the viewing taking place in 5,100 homes from the 25 million or more,[82] carefully selected to reflect the changing patterns of life in Britain. In all, some 11,500 viewers are included, from a population approaching 60 million, which is statistically a reliable sample. Much of the information is collected automatically. All the sets in the household are metered to record information about how they have been used (to view a TV channel, a DVD or VHS recorded off-air, or to play a game, etc), when and for how long. Handsets resembling a remote control allow the household to record who is watching, including visitors. All the information collected is downloaded automatically to BARB between 2am and 6am, and the first results are on the desks of senior TV and advertising executives around 10am the following morning. These are the 'overnights', which give a headline figure of the number of people who watched. These are refined in the next seven days to produce a detailed demographic and regional breakdown, which will also include timeshifted viewing on VHS, DVD, PVR or other devices. The figures can then be processed in many different ways, from providing a simple top 100 of most-viewed programmes to analysing minute-by-minute the shifting composition of the viewing audience for a particular programme.

The figures have had a remarkable influence on the decisions of broadcasters. They provide the principal, if not the only, means of understanding the audience as a whole. They provide almost instant confirmation that a new programme has performed as expected, and evidence after a few days of the possible reasons for the failures. As TV has become more conscious of marketing issues, the demographics have been used to identify the kinds of people who are not being offered much that might appeal to them in particular timeslots, and so to devise programmes to suit their presumed tastes. Since the late 1980s, 'the ratings' in the UK have determined the planning of new programmes, the revision of existing ones and the construction of the schedule.»

Q39 Does TV exist to sell audiences to advertisers?

Other measures of the audience also exist. The longest established is what is now known as the 'Appreciation Index' ('the AIs'), which evolved from the earliest forms of radio audience survey undertaken by the BBC during the 1930s, well before the days of ratings. The survey, however, is not routinely made available, unlike BARB's basic figures, which are published weekly in the pages of the trade magazine *Broadcast*, and on BARB's own website. The AIs simply rate on a scale of 1–100 the amount that viewers had appreciated a programme. Unlike BARB's automated data collection, these rely on various forms of face-to-face polling, phone interviews and questionnaires. The levels of appreciation tend to bunch between 65 and 85 or, as William G. Stewart recounts from the 1960s, 'for sitcoms (*Sykes*, *Hancock*, *Harry Worth*) an AI of 70–75 was fine. Anything below that meant long faces; anything around 80 would be dropped into the conversation at the BBC Club at lunchtime.'[83] BBC Two Controller Jane Root claimed, on her departure, that 'Last summer on BBC Two we showed a late night programme about astronomy, working with the Open University. Not that many people watched it, no one reviewed it – it was the middle of the night – but those who did see it were really passionate about it. It got the highest AI score of the week.' She then elaborated: 'The AI, the audience appreciation index, tells us the extent to which people value the programmes they watch. Not just that they are in the room.'[84]

The ratings system has served the era of mass broadcasting relatively well, by giving a wholesale view of TV. It measures, as Root points out, how many people are in the room but not what impact the programme is making on them. The continuing existence of the Appreciation Index is the clearest indication that some broadcasters are unhappy with the ratings system, but have been in a minority. The digital era is changing that. With the diversification of ways of getting access to programmes, the question of their value to their viewers becomes more relevant. With increasing choice not only of programmes but of ways of watching, the certainties that underpin the ratings are eroding fast.

The BBC has proposed a number of alternative measures of audience satisfaction which, unsurprisingly, relate particularly to the public role of broadcast programmes. They include memorability, points of impact beyond broadcasting, approval, innovation, impartiality, trust and peer review, as well as the Appreciation Index and the size of the audience. In its policy document 'Building Public Value',[85] the BBC begins to explore this bewildering series of possible measures. They include issues that relate to the reputation of programmes within the TV industry like 'peer review' and 'innovation', which could be assessed by a panel of critics and fellow programme-makers. There are relatively subjective indicators that can be assessed relatively quickly after broadcast (approval, impartiality, trust and appreciation), which would require careful audience interviews rather than a tick-box questionnaire. Then there is a category which looks at more long-term impact: memorability and impact beyond broadcasting. This last indicates the general influence that a programme might have had. For the BBC, this would be the impact on wider activity of, for instance, *Book Week* on BBC Two (leading to greater book sales and public library loans); the use of the programme in teaching; the activity of a viewer in accessing the programme website or sending their own footage to it; or even its subsequent sale on DVD. For an advertiser, impact beyond broadcasting might mean a rise in sales or increased recognition of their brand.

This list of possible indicators is, even in a historic moment dominated by 'performance indicators', a formidable range of measurements of the success of a particular programme. A further perspective should be added, that of how much and how intensely audience members use various media. This would include not only their TV viewing but also what other media they use, how much, and how intently. Many people watch TV while using other media,**»** so the style and the intensity of watching has a crucial impact on how much they value the programmes they watch.

There are many potential ways of understanding the TV audience and its relation to programmes. Indeed, the singular word 'audience' is actively misleading as a way

Q11

» Q2

of understanding what happens at the receiving end of broadcasting and the wider circulation of a TV programme. New-screen activities» have eroded the wholesale certainties underlying the ratings system. Equally, they have eroded the market for the traditional thirty-second TV spot advert which was the original reason for the reliance on a marketer's view of viewers.»

» Q42

Why aren't there any ads on the BBC?

Advertising is pervasive on TV and the Internet. So the BBC's lack of advertising is ever more remarkable. It has its roots in beliefs about the relationship between broadcasting and society which have changed over the eighty or so years since the idea was first formed. Whilst the thinking may have changed, the peculiar convenience of TV without adverts has remained a consistent feature of UK broadcasting and a model for other democratic nations as well. Occasionally, as in the late 1980s, the attack on the idea has been so sustained and universal that its days have seemed numbered, but in 2006 the BBC's Charter was renewed for another ten years, guaranteeing an advert-free TV service for as long as anyone can anticipate the future life of broadcast TV.

The BBC began broadcasting radio in the 1920s (it introduced TV in 1936), and the spectre of 'how they do things in America' was at the forefront of the then government's mind. Radio in the USA had begun as a joyous free-for-all, with all and any kind of message and music being broadcast, with a heavy dose of advertising to support it. In the early days of US radio, it seemed quite natural that advertisers should have a considerable degree of control over the content of broadcasting.

The thinking of the British political establishment was altogether different. Just emerging from a traumatic world war, they saw radio as a means of educating the population as well as entertaining them. They developed the idea of a benevolent monopoly broadcaster which would be free from both commercial and direct political influence. From the desire to avoid the anarchy and unrestrained commercialism of the USA was born a model known as 'public service broadcasting'. Broadcasting was conceived as a public good, above both the half-truths of the market and the hurly-burly of party politics. It would provide citizens with information about their society and would actively help in developing a more cultured and socially minded population. The service would be paid for by a licence on the ownership of radio sets rather than by advertisements that listeners were compelled to hear. Political neutrality would be guaranteed by a Board of Governors who would ensure that the organisation remained both well run and politically impartial.

That was the idealism that gave birth to a BBC that carried no advertising. It also gave birth to a BBC that was relatively autonomous from government. However, the government had three substantial means to control the BBC, all of which have been used by successive governments since the initial charter was granted in 1926. The first is the periodic requirement to renew the BBC's Charter, an event that takes place once a decade or so, and provokes substantial debate about the BBC's role and its performance of it. The second is the right to set the level of the licence fee. This was used after John Birt's appointment as Director-General in 1992 to set the BBC's income below the level of inflation and thus bring about substantial reforms in its way of working. The third is to appoint governors or even chairs of governors who are hostile to the BBC's activities, as was done with Lord Hill in 1967 (by Labour Prime Minister Harold Wilson) and in 1986 with Marmaduke Hussey (by Conservative Prime Minister Margaret Thatcher). In any case, the BBC's decision to support the government during the General Strike of 1926 was a founding gesture that indicated that it would be an organisation that would, in a crisis, suspend its independence in favour of supporting the existing structure of the state and those running it at the time.

The political independence of the BBC was a fragile thing from the start. But its independence from commercial influence has been a more robustly defended principle until recently. There were a few voices in commercial broadcasting who have complained stridently about the privileged status of the BBC, but many of their colleagues used to point out that an advertising-free BBC restricted the amount of TV available as advertising space and so drove up the prices that ITV could command. However, this balance of power began to change when more broadcasting channels became available during the 1980s.

Famously, the media tycoon Rupert Murdoch declared that 'public-service broadcasting should serve the public what they want' without regard to wider issues of the role of broadcasting in society. The BBC was accused of 'distorting the market' and public-service broadcasting was increasingly regarded as an old-fashioned concept in an era of increasing sophistication and choice.

The economist Andrew Graham has produced an elegant justification of public-service broadcasting in terms which address, rather than dismiss, the existence of a market economy.[86] He argues that citizenship 'in liberal societies, entails a range of rights beyond the mere casting of votes'. He identifies three such rights that are the particular concern of media: the right to information about 'how society is governed, what are the laws of the land, who represents you'; the right to equality of respect, which he defines in terms of the ability of different sections of society to represent themselves and to be represented in a fair way; and the right to participate in society through forms of political engagement. He asserts that 'these are not the concern of the market nor are they of commercial broadcasters' and, further, that 'for these rights to have meaning, such information should be free and not sold for profit'. This links with many other defences of public-service broadcasting down the years.

However, Graham then takes the argument to the enemy's terrain, as it were: the theory of the primacy of the market and the sovereignty of consumer choice. 'It is often forgotten that the theory of choice, on which rest the claims for a free market in broadcasting, presupposes consumers who are already both fully formed – they know their own preferences – and fully informed. In reality, neither is likely.' For a market to function, it is necessary that the individuals who are both buying and selling should have access to reliable information so that the market can work properly. According to economists, perfect markets require perfect access to all information, a perfect state which economists know perfectly well cannot exist. Nevertheless, some degree of reliable information is needed for the basic functioning of markets, so that

Q40 Why aren't there any ads on the BBC?

buyers and sellers can find one another, sellers can set prices and so that some generally known level of trust (or 'custom and practice') can underpin its interactions.

Graham argues that if information is a prerequisite for the function of markets, then it cannot be treated as a market commodity like any other. Information cannot simply be bought and sold on the market. There has to be reliable information that is universally accessible so that markets can exist at all. Therefore, Graham argues, government must make sure that such information does exist. Hence government has a continuing role in regulating TV broadcasting. He asserts that 'the existence of a set of broadcasters committed to empowering citizens and providing impartial information increases the autonomy of the individual – and without this autonomy, where is the real choice?'

'Information' in the sense used here is not limited to programmes which tell audiences about things. Early public-service broadcasting gained a reputation for such programmes, with the BBC being nicknamed 'Auntie' and lampooned for the serious, lecturing tone of much of its output. This may well have been appropriate for the early period of broadcasting and the restrained circumstances of post-war Britain, but it began to fall away in the 1960s with the development of more and more programming that mixed information and entertainment. The current BBC counts its main soap opera *EastEnders* amongst such programming, and argues that many of its dramas provide
» Q21   insight into fellow human beings.**»** Such is the argument of this book as well.

There are no adverts on the BBC because the BBC is conceived as a public-service broadcaster. It is constituted to serve a number of 'public purposes' through the provision of entertainment and information that is not influenced by concerns of advertising. In doing so, it continues to influence the wider broadcasting market in the UK. But its privileged position carries with it responsibilities and dangers. The responsibilities are those of acting in a democratic and open way which often conflict with the demands of entertainment or of news exclusivity. It also carries the dangers of continuing dependence on government and thus of being forced to bend to a government's will. An advertising-free BBC is in itself therefore no guarantee of impartial information. It requires a continuing awareness of why the BBC exists as it does, and a political and social agreement that such an institution should remain an important feature of UK society.

How can I get a job in TV?

'**How can I get** a job in TV?' is perhaps the most frequently asked question of all, as the TV industry has a glamorous aura. The reality, for most who work in it, is different. TV workers work longer hours than average and the majority are freelance or on short contracts. In the UK, media workers work an average of 44.6 hours a week. Many jobs involve unsocial hours, and so it is not surprising that there is a preponderance of younger people working in TV. In the UK, half are under 35, whereas only thirty-six per cent of the UK workforce falls into that age group, and only fifteen per cent of TV workers are over fifty, as against twenty-six per cent of the total workforce.[87] This is a stressful industry in which burn-out is common. Yet still there are more people wanting jobs in TV than there are jobs available.

The TV industry is small compared to its social visibility and importance. As the number of channels has grown, there has not been a proportionate growth of jobs in the creation of programming or in the direct administration of TV channels. Technological changes mean that the number of such jobs increased slowly as many tasks have become simpler or more automated. Grades such as 'assistant editor' have disappeared with the universal use of digital editing. New technical specialisms have emerged, from colourists to reversioners, reflecting the potential of new technologies. However, these roles have not added appreciably to the total employed. The one area of growth has been in the administration of the more complex systems of channel delivery: in cable and satellite subscription services and their call centres, in the back-office legal areas like the administration of rights, and in new-screen opportunities taken up by broadcasters.

Direct employment in TV remains the privilege of a minority of the population, so it is no surprise that sixty-nine per cent of people working in TV have a university degree, compared to just fifteen per cent of the UK population as a whole. Of these degree holders, forty-four per cent have studied media for their degree.[88] TV is still, therefore, an elite occupation. The size of that group is difficult to work out precisely: many of those involved in TV work can and do work in many other media as well, from newspapers to live theatre (journalists or actors for instance). Omitting such people who are a key part of TV but who routinely move between media in their work, it is possible to gauge the size of the working group that includes everyone from commissioning editors, producers and directors to camera assistants, specialist make-up artists and set-builders.

The training organisation Skillset's 2005 census of this workforce that derives income from working with moving images and sound is some 112,200 in the UK.[89] This number was derived from a snapshot survey of one working day, which revealed a reserve army of some 50,000 freelancers amongst them, waiting for work but not actually working. This group represents a little less than 0.4 per cent of the working population in the UK.[90] Even then, many of them find work for their specialist roles for other media as well. Many editors will be working on material for movies, commercials, corporate productions and the games industry; those in special effects will work more for movies and commercials than they do for TV. So it is likely that the broadcast industry in the UK is routinely employing around 60,000 people at best,[91] apart from its journalists and performers; that is something like two people in every thousand who are working in the UK.

Surprisingly, the statistics for the USA are roughly similar. According to the US Department of Labor, the broadcasting industry employed 127,500 people in May 2005, and the whole of the motion picture and sound production another 386,890. This group together represented around 0.35 per cent of the working population of the USA in May 2005.[92] These figures represents 'behind the camera', technical and administrative roles and not journalists or performers. That group is somewhat larger: in 1999, there were some 46,000 TV and radio announcers in the USA.[93] In the UK in 2006, an estimated 76,000 people worked as journalists, of whom 47,000 had full-time jobs. For the 38,000 people

Q41 How can I get a job in TV?

who were actors, the prospect of work was less good.[94] The estimate of the proportion of actors out of work (or 'resting') at any particular time was ninety per cent. So even if these two professions are included in the figures of total jobs within the TV industry, it still remains much smaller than its influence or its cultural visibility would imply.

Such an industry can pick and choose who its employees. It requires a high level of skill. Clearly a university degree – but not necessarily in a media-related subject – is a prerequisite. Everything else depends on fulfilling the requirements of employers who tend to require highly skilled staff at short notice. They will want these staff to be able to work as part of a rapidly assembled team working under pressure. They will therefore be looking for people who already have the desired skills, with whom they have worked before or those of their workforce they want to promote, or those who come with recommendations from a trusted source. Despite attempts by the media industry training agency Skillset, there are still no standard skills qualifications in the TV industry, and if there were it is likely that many would be outdated as soon as the first workers had qualified for them. So contacts, word of mouth and a good track record are all important indicators for prospective employers.

Track record depends on getting established within the TV industry, or moving across from an allied media industry where employment is easier to find. Many production companies offer 'work experience' for those who are in, or have recently left, education. Depending on the nature of the company, such unpaid posts can be a valuable way of entering the industry, or indeed of finding out that it is not after all a work environment that you want to inhabit. Unpaid work placements should at least pay travelling expenses, and should have a limited time span and the possibility of becoming a paid employee at the end of the period. However, some companies use such workers as a way of boosting profits or even of staying afloat, relying on the skills and enthusiasm of those in work placement to complete projects. There is also what

Skillset refer to as 'the low/no budget end of things'.[95] This can provide valuable experience of the difficulties of production, and it might provide material for a showreel. However, zero-budget productions can often fail to impress unless the underlying idea is strong.

Despite its image and the number of people who want to work in it, TV production is by no means glamorous. Besides long hours, it involves a great deal of repetitive work,» and, for those who are in more creative roles, a great deal of frustration. Considerable work and time goes into the development of projects which never find a commission. Even more work goes into those which are produced but are cancelled by their initial broadcaster or are sidelined into an obscure part of the schedule. However, the rewards of success are considerable as broadcasting is still an elite sector of the cultural industries.

Q41 How can I get a job in TV?

Who pays for TV?

The people who watch TV have always paid for it, but mostly they have not noticed that they are doing so. The reason why TV grew into such a pervasive medium was because, once a set had been bought or hired, watching it involved no further expense apart from paying the licence fee. Three ways of financing TV were developed during TV's first decades. The first was simply to sell advertising space between or even within programmes. The second was to levy a licence fee which paid more or less directly for a monopoly TV broadcaster. The third, in emergent nations, was to fund TV directly from taxes both as a means of propaganda and as a symbol of being a modern state.

Some nations have successfully mixed all three models as is the case in the Netherlands. Broadcast time was allocated to independent suppliers aligned with major Dutch social or religious groups, in proportion to the number of subscribers to their programme magazine, which became a way of expressing support. Each supplying broadcaster was allocated income from the licence fee which could be supplemented by advertising. The Dutch system had the advantage of expressing some kind of direct relationship with the broadcaster, through affiliation with a group. But in general the relationship between viewer payment and the services they received was at best indirect, as with the licence fee. In the case of advertising, it was so indirect as to be imperceptible. This first phase of television could even be said to have been funded from a series of taxes on consumption in general rather than from any direct 'paying customer' kind of relationship.

During the 1980s, a more direct model of viewer payment developed with the new technologies of satellite and cable. This saw the emergence of subscription-based services like HBO (Home Box Office) in the USA as well as multichannel suppliers like Sky providing different packages of channels for different levels of payment. Even here, there is still no direct relationship between what a viewer wants and what they pay for. Subscription to a package of channels is now a commonplace activity, but that still involves paying for many programmes that the subscriber will not watch and may not even want to watch. Payment on a programme-by-programme basis has not yet established itself in broadcasting. Apart from payment for 'premium' sports events (special events surrounded by a high level of anticipation), pay-per-view scarcely exists.

Another means of getting money from viewers has been developed by those that have a high level of interaction with their audiences. The income from people phoning in to try to become contestants in the quiz show *Who Wants to Be a Millionaire?* more or less pays for the prize money that is paid out. SMS texted or phoned-in votes for *Big Brother* contestants provide significant income to the producers and broadcasters. Interaction comes at a price in TV, and further income can sometimes be gained from other activity like spin-off products. Useful as it is for particular formats, it is not a system that could sustain TV broadcasting as a whole.

Advertising-funded broadcasting still predominates. The majority of advertising takes the form of the spot advert in breaks within programmes or in the gaps between them. Traditionally, advertising breaks in programmes have been at worst a mild irritation, and at best a convenient break for other pressing domestic activities. However, things are not that simple. A number of serious problems for broadcasting result from the prevalence of advertiser-funded broadcasting, and the diversification of TV and new-screen activities means that the arrangement is, if not doomed, then certainly destined to change fundamentally. This will cause particular problems for channels like Channel 4, which has been able, since 1990, to support its explicitly minority and innovative programming on the basis of a buoyant market for TV advertising.

Advertising has the great advantage of providing free TV for millions, paid for from the marketing budgets of products that they buy every day. Normally in groups of half-minute adverts in programme breaks, TV advertising was successful because of the scarcity of other mass-advertising media. When television arrived it offered something unique: the ability to use moving images and sounds to reach an audience numbered in the millions. For a particular phase of economic development, this was a perfect tool. The market for standard everyday commodities was set to grow exponentially in the UK of the late 1950s, and TV offered the ideal place to show what these everyday products were, how they should be used and how they would improve life immeasurably. They could show soap powder, custard powder, flea powder, carpet powder; chocolate powder, chocolate bars, chocolate sauce; OK sauce, Daddy's sauce, HP sauce; Bisto, Oxo, Omo. Television advertising was central to developing the market for fast-moving consumer goods.

Most of these everyday items have disappeared from regular TV advertising. Manufacturers have found that other media provide more convenient forms of promotion. One of these is the point of sale itself, which has mutated to produce standard supermarket chains as the predominant means of buying such goods. TV advertising of individual everyday products is reserved for new launches and relaunches rather than the everyday activity of keeping the brand before the public. TV has become the arena of competition between the supermarket brands themselves, with celebrity chef Jamie Oliver fronting for Sainsburys; Marks and Spencer claiming that 'this is not ordinary food: this is Marks and Spencer food', and Morrison's stressing their 'buy one, get one free' offers. The spot advert as a fundamental funding source for TV in the future is under threat from two sides: the rise of other media like the Internet, and the increasing ability of viewers to ignore or skip them entirely.

The spot advert always had some disadvantages as a form of paying for TV. It tends to skew the demographic address of programmes towards those population groups

» Q39

who are of most interest to advertisers.» There is an inherent unpredictability in the market for advertising, which often anticipates both downturns and upturns in the overall economy, leading the TV industry to be out of step with the mainstream of economic activity. Finally, there is

TV FAQ

a feeling that somehow it is plain wrong that a universal cultural activity like TV should be so subject to the whims of a particular sector of society, the advertising industry. So the form of public-service broadcasting, usually funded by a licence fee, continues in many European countries to provide a counterbalance to these tendencies in advertiser-funded TV.»

Q40

The presence of a public-service broadcaster like the BBC can have the effect of bringing some diversity into the market. Public-service broadcasters can produce programming that is not initially appealing to advertisers, so maintaining their position in the affection of audiences. Where a public-service channel is confident and relatively free from direct political control, this can provide a force for innovation in TV. This was the case with documentaries in the UK, which disappeared from ITV almost completely in the early 1980s. The BBC maintained some documentary production which led to the development of a new, popular, documentary format, the docusoap. Although virtually abandoned by the BBC by 2005, this format still provided an early-evening staple for the commercial channel ITV in the form of series like *Airport*.

Broadcasting in the UK has long been regulated on the principle that a diversity of funding is more likely to provide a diversity of programming.» Current developments seem to prove the wisdom of this approach. New technologies are breaking up the seamless flow of broadcasting, making it much easier for viewers to avoid spot ads completely. So the market for such advertising is under pressure as never before. Major consumer brands like Heinz have simply abandoned TV advertising all together. The spot advertisement is under threat as a way of paying for TV. But no clear replacement seems to exist.

Q43

TV is deeply ingrained culturally as a medium that has separated the moments of payment and viewing. As a result, TV has offered the possibility of the casual encounter with both programmes and advertising. There is nothing to be paid for just taking a look, for browsing or watching several programmes at the same time by flipping between them. There is no direct consumer relationship in

Q42 Who pays for TV?

the market for TV programmes as there is in the cinema. The box-office performance of a particular film defines its subsequent value in different forms of distribution like DVD sale, and indeed its importance when screened on TV. Similarly, new-screen distribution outlets for moving image and sound, like downloads or streaming, viewing over mobile phones and other such devices, are all trying to build pay-per-view means of financing.

Yet TV programmes do not enter such a marketplace. Instead their success or failure is judged by 'the ratings' or audience figures and, sometimes, other forms of evaluation

» 039 like the audience Appreciation Index.» Commercial broadcasters sell advertising to pay for the programmes, and those that have been most successful in ratings terms command a premium in the market. This might seem surprising as it is usual to pay to see a film in a cinema, to obtain a DVD or book, and even to pay for a download. However, there remains something distinctive about TV. It is a service rather than a purchase, available whenever wanted rather than bought only when required.

Sponsorship seems to offer one solution to the decline in income from spot advertising. It is a more sophisticated form of advertising, in which an advertiser can associate their brand or product with a particular programme. In the USA, this is taken to the extent that a single sponsor can pay for the entire production of a programme. The term 'soap opera', for instance, comes from the activity of soap manufacturer Proctor and Gamble as the actual producer of radio programmes in the 1930s. In TV sponsorship, it is more usual for the sponsor to pay a specialised production company to make programmes, creating a three-way relationship between sponsor, producer and broadcaster that is sometimes difficult to negotiate. The film *Goodnight and Good Luck* vividly shows the strains of such a relationship, where the broadcaster defended Murrow's crucial broadcasts against Senator Joe McCarthy, but responded to sponsor pressure by progressively reducing Murrow's editorial freedom and choice of topic thereafter. Indeed, as rising programme costs forced the US system to move to multiple sponsorship of individual shows after the mid 1950s, the desire to offend no potential sponsors at all produced a general avoidance of controversy.

When the UK parliament introduced commercial broadcasting in 1955, sponsorship was rejected in favour of the spot advert. Sponsorship has since been introduced gradually by the regulators as another consequence of the multiplication of channels in the late 1980s. A series of editorial test cases defined an 'arm's length' relationship between sponsor and programme. So the chocolate company Cadbury sponsored the ITV soap opera *Coronation Street* for ten years between 1996 and 2006, but had no direct input into stories or other issues around the series. Instead, it created a product association: the comfort of Cadbury's chocolates with the familiarity of *Coronation Street*. This was a relatively easy relationship to build since *Coronation Street* is a well-known cultural icon. The sponsorship relationship gave Cadbury advertising space at the beginning and end of each programme and at each break. The association between Cadbury and the series integrated Cadbury images into the run and feel of the programme itself in ingenious ways using chocolate figures of the *Street*'s main characters, created by Aardman Animation. Other sponsorship models can involve the sponsorship by a brand of an entire genre of programming on a channel, like the relationship between the phone directory enquiries brand 118 and the drama output of Channel 4.

However, sponsorship is not enough on its own. The number of available relationships between programmes and brands is low compared to the number of potential advertisers. So a further means of funding is gaining ground: product placement. Though commonplace in movie production and US television, product placement has no official place in the funding structures of European broadcasting. It is a simple principle. Instead of showing off products in breaks within programmes, the products are put into the programmes themselves. The producers of the programmes and the broadcasters are paid a substantial amount for showing products in this way.

Since any drama or even documentary in a contemporary setting will naturally require everyday products, there might seem to be no particular problem with such an arrangement. Indeed, it would be artificial to avoid displaying any product brands in such a programme as such logos are pervasive in modern domestic and public spaces. The BBC once tried to avoid displaying any brands in its productions, but has had to concede on this issue. The organisation still makes a spirited attempt to avoid known brand names, or even to invent them where possible, but even the most inattentive viewer is aware of the advertising hoardings whose constant motion is a distraction in the background of any sporting event. As products are naturally placed in TV images anyway, it might seem that there is no harm in TV gaining revenue from them.

Those who argue against the spread of product placement point to the same problems as those of any advertiser-funded service: the skewing of demographics and the possibility of undue influence on content. It is unlikely, for example, that a car manufacturer would place their vehicles in a drama involving accidents caused by faulty cars. However, an arrangement might perhaps be reached in which the faulty vehicles were manufactured by a competitor. Such are the editorial problems of product placement, which can be resolved only by the growth of an even more savvy and cynical viewing audience who assume that products are included in dramas because someone has paid to put them there. And that might well undermine the whole point of doing so, unless the aim is a more diffuse sense of brand and product awareness.

The problem of who pays for TV continues. In the end it is TV viewers who pay, directly or indirectly. However, for as long as TV is a service rather than a set of single programme sales, it is likely that most TV services will be supported by an increasingly complex mixture of different streams of income. Premium events will be available for subscribers or pay-per-view customers who will get them first on premium channels. Subscription channels will showcase material on free-to-view channels to attract subscribers. Production budgets will be underwritten by product-placement arrangements which will remain practically invisible to viewers, and by substantial charges for voting and other forms of viewer participation. On-screen sponsorship deals will proliferate, and spot advertising will become more of an entertainment form in its own right. Additional income will be derived from phone-in participation, advice services and spin-off products. New-screen means of accessing broadcast content will provide further income as the operators of mobile phone companies and download sites will be able to charge on a pay-per-view basis. They will compete to be able to use the distinctive brands of broadcast content as a way of promoting their services.**»** Licence-fee funding will continue at least until the emerging forms of payment have shown what level of TV they can sustain. It may well be that the licence fee or its equivalent will prove to be the easiest way of maintaining a minimum universal TV service.

Q37

Who regulates TV... and why?

From the beginning, the TV industry has been regulated for two reasons. First, it brought a new kind of content into people's homes and, second, it offered a new means of communication with clear political and social power. Content regulation recognised that TV's role as a domestic and universal medium posed some major problems for many sections of the population in terms of seeing things of which they disapproved or which shocked and horrified them. TV allowed the population in general to see into the lives of others, seeing and hearing things that they would rather ignore or even things of which they had hitherto been unaware. Regulation would arbitrate between society's need to know and the desire of many not to know.

The issue of the political and social power of the medium means that individual politicians or whole governments sometimes try to change what broadcasters are saying, particularly at times of great political controversy. Otherwise, the detailed regulation of broadcasting is delegated by governments to separate bodies with varying degrees of independence. The detailed regulation of broadcasting is further complicated by the scarcity of TV as a resource, and the expense and difficulty of setting up any TV service. There continue to be physical limits on the number of wavelengths that can be used for broadcasting. Whereas some means of broadcasting have a near universal reach, others do not, so TV broadcasting is almost universally regarded as a public asset to be allocated and regulated, rather than something that anyone can just grab.

Behind both of these issues of content and power lies the fundamental question of the place of TV in market economies as a purveyor of basic information about the world. As Andrew Graham argues, this makes TV more than just an industry.**»** The right to broadcast has been

» Q40

seen as a public asset, which is licensed to commercial companies on certain conditions. In countries like Britain, this regulation historically has included the requirement to separate advertising from programmes, to make and show particular kinds of programmes whether religious, news or factual, and to abide by detailed guidelines on taste, decency and objectivity.

These conditions were required of the companies operating licences for the first commercial channel ITV when it was set up in 1955, of Channel 4 when it opened in 1982, and of Channel 5 from 1997. They were policed by a regulatory body which lasted in various manifestations (the Independent Television Authority, the Independent Broadcasting Authority, etc). This body was also responsible for the allocation of the right to broadcast, first by vetting candidates thoroughly, latterly by an open bidding process. The ITA/IBA/ITC was subsumed into the overall telecoms regulator Ofcom in 2003, when commercial TV was subjected to a more liberal, but still significant, regime of regulation.

The regulation of programmes has several aspects, of which the regulatory bodies are just one. Regulation is carried out both through the general laws governing communications media and by specific regulatory organisations which are responsible both for programmes and for the allocation of wavelength franchises to broadcasters. A series of laws, specific and different in every country, govern what broadcast and other media are able to say about individuals and organisations: laws relating to libel and defamation. Many countries also have legislation that prevents the media from incitement to racial hatred for example. As broadcasting becomes more diverse, the long-term tendency of broadcast-content regulation is to use general legislation to regulate what is shown, rather than to let specific regulating bodies grow ever larger. However, there still exist several areas in which broadcasting is subject to more stringent controls which are administered through or overseen by the regulators, as well as the subject of self-censorship by broadcasting professionals and broadcasting companies.

In Britain, there is a particular concern with portrayals of violence, even within news; with explicit portrayals of nudity and sexual activity; with offensive behaviour including blasphemous criticism of religions; and with inappropriate

Q43 Who regulates TV... and why?

language, especially swearing. Indeed, many surveys have shown that 'bad language' is the issue of greatest concern in the UK. These concerns result from the domestic nature of TV, and the fact that it is capable of bringing unwanted images and sounds into the home from outside. They also result from the nature of broadcasting as an inclusive and indiscriminate medium, available to all and every one of the population. TV's universality means that it is likely to offend substantial sections of the population unless it remains completely anodyne. The more easily shocked are often mobilised into pressure groups like mediawatch-uk, the successor to Mary Whitehouse's moralistic National Viewers and Listeners Association.

The routine regulation of programme content is carried out by broadcast professionals in every decision they make. Formal regulation, either by laws or by the statutory regulatory body, is a sign that this process of self-regulation has gone wrong, or, more rarely, that social attitudes are changing faster than broadcasters realise. Self-regulation is carried out partly through the spontaneous expression of the personal preferences of the broadcast professionals themselves, who will want to avoid some issues or forms of expression. Such general, unthinking, cultural bias is an aspect of any system, but such attitudes are continually challenged in the constant search for novel subjects and fresh means of expression.

In addition, individual judgements in sensitive areas are measured against general sets of rules. Every major UK broadcaster produces codes of conduct for internal use. These are often modelled on the BBC's very detailed Editorial Guidelines, which the BBC now makes available in a constantly updated online form.[96] They contain guidance or instructions on every controversial issue that broadcasters might cover, from alcohol abuse to the coverage of young people. They include sections on harm and offence and impartiality, as well as the many difficult moral issues that reporters are likely to encounter.» The section on 'War Terror and Emergencies' includes the guidelines that:

» Q6, Q10

We should respect human dignity without sanitising the realities of war. There must be clear editorial justification for the use of very graphic pictures of war or atrocity

and

We will ensure, as far as is reasonably possible, that next of kin do not learn of a person's death or injury from our news bulletins, websites or programmes.[97]

These two guidelines between them ensure that the BBC tends to show fewer victims of atrocities than broadcasters in other countries. Other UK news providers tend to follow the BBC's lead on this question, giving UK audiences a different view of war and terror attacks (and even major accidents) to those shown to audiences elsewhere.**》** The BBC guidelines also explain the basic principle of self-regulation employed by broadcasters, the idea of 'referral up'. Where a producer feels that they are 'taking a risk' with a controversial item, even a line of dialogue, it is standard practice to ask a more senior manager for approval. This builds in a certain level of collective caution, and the guidelines reinforce this by detailing those areas where 'mandatory referral' is required. Asking your superiors tends to be the general principle of internal regulation within broadcasting.

External regulators intervene mainly when these internal procedures have broken down. Apart from the BBC, which has had a long history of self-management, broadcasting in the UK has been regulated the Independent Television Authority (ITA) and its successor bodies and now Ofcom. Ofcom allocates broadcasting frequencies and intervenes in commercial matters. It takes a less interventionist role on issues of content than did the IBA, which for many years used its right to view controversial programmes before their broadcast, and, if it wished, demand changes or ban them entirely.

Ofcom no longer has such a right, although it can censure

Q43 Who regulates TV... and why?

broadcasters if their internal regulation processes have not worked to Ofcom's mandatory code of conduct. The focus of this code 'is on adult audiences making informed choices within a regulatory framework which gives them a reasonable expectation of what they will receive, while at the same time robustly protecting those too young to exercise fully informed choices for themselves'.[98] This is a new emphasis in the regulation of TV in the UK, and clearly indicates that Ofcom regards viewer choice as part of the process of regulation, in line with the more liberal free-market view that Ofcom is adopting in relation to telecommunications. Nonetheless, there is a significant exception made in relation to 'those too young to exercise fully informed choices for themselves'. Protection of children from certain kinds of content (violent or sexual in the main) is a constant theme in TV regulation because of the domestic nature of TV. In this case, it indicates that, for instance, Ofcom intends to maintain the rule that content of an adult nature can be broadcast only after the 9pm 'watershed', a well-established scheduling principle**》** that is widely recognised by viewers.

》 038

But Ofcom and its equivalent bodies in other countries are not the only organisations that can and do censor TV broadcasts. Both individuals and lobbying groups or large corporations can use the law courts to request an injunction preventing a programme from being broadcast if they can convince the courts that it will be harmful to them as individuals or will otherwise break the law. But the most controversial form of intervention is the directly political attempts at censorship that are sometimes undertaken by politicians. In 2004, one such attempt led to a fundamental change in the way that the BBC regulates its affairs.

The BBC's guidelines are the product of the BBC's long history of self-regulation, which was the basis for its editorial independence from direct political intervention in what it broadcast. The BBC's governors, appointed by government and drawn overwhelmingly from outside broadcasting, were meant to both defend the editorial independence of the organisation and oversee its management. This proved increasingly difficult in the face of attempts made by governments to challenge the BBC's editorial independence. Several attempts were made in the 1980s by the then Conservative government, but the intervention of Tony Blair's Labour government between 2003 and 2004 had more long-term consequences.

In the sensitive time leading up to the Anglo-American invasion of Iraq, a BBC defence correspondent, Andrew Gilligan, alleged that the Prime Minister's team had 'sexed up' the intelligence service evidence in their dossier arguing that Iraq had weapons of mass destruction. He cited a reliable source who turned out to be intelligence expert Dr David Kelly. Once unmasked (by the Ministry of Defence, not the BBC), Dr Kelly committed suicide. It emerged that he did not quite say what Gilligan said that he had said. Events in general have proved that Gilligan was broadly right, but in journalism being generally right and proving an allegation are necessarily different. Instead of backing down on Gilligan's loose wording, the BBC leapt to a wholesale defence of the report. At the time, their reporting of widespread protests about the impending invasion of Iraq was the target of daily intimidating calls and messages from Downing Street's then Director of Communications, Alastair Campbell. It may well be that the staunch defence of Gilligan was seen as a way of facing down the government. However, events became graver with Dr Kelly's suicide, and a judge, Lord Hutton, was commissioned to conduct a public inquiry into the affair. For many weeks, the public were treated to a rare insight into the duplicity of politicians and the mysteries of the intelligence service as the evidence was made public.

In January 2004, Lord Hutton concluded, against general opinion, that the government was incapable of lying and that the BBC had broken its guidelines by broadcasting Gilligan's inaccurate account of Kelly's words. The Chairman of the BBC Board of Governors, Gavyn Davies, immediately resigned, and the remaining governors forced the Director-General, Greg Dyke, to quit as well.[99] The BBC was left without a chairman and a director-general for the first time in its history. This was the second time in twenty years that the Board of Governors had caved in to government pressure, the first being the *Real Lives* affair in 1985, when the governors overruled their Director-General, Alasdair Milne, and prevented the transmission of a programme about Northern Ireland.[100] As a result of the Gilligan affair, the role of the governors was widely questioned in the press as they seemed to be incapable of defending the BBC against direct political interference. Even the Labour government recognised that the governors had acted more cravenly than they had expected, and that this damaged the trust that the BBC could command, both in the UK and around the world.» This damage to the BBC brand» was not a result that the government had wanted, as the BBC plays an important role as a trusted news provider around the world both through its global broadcasting and its news website.

» Q5
» Q37

So the role of the BBC governors was rethought. At the beginning of 2007, a new form of governance was introduced, which separated the management and the regulation functions of the governors. The BBC Executive Board would now be responsible for the running of the organisation, and a separate BBC Trust would regulate many of its activities. The initial appointments to the Trust were of a different character to the outgoing Board of Governors, as they included experienced broadcasters for the first time. However, Ofcom is now involved in some of the work of this Trust, particularly in regulating the overall market impact of new BBC business initiatives through a 'Public Value Test'. In essence, this is a new form of economic regulation of the BBC, which seeks to limit its activities to those which can be shown to accord with its public-service rationale.»

» Q40

The regulation of TV involves many different factors, from the routine self-censorship practised by broadcasting professionals, through various formal mechanisms of regulation and the legal system, to the tough and wayward world of political intervention. Regulation involves discussion and rules about programme content and the scheduling of programmes. It involves an economic analysis of the broadcasting industry; the decision on who can be allocated the right to broadcast at what price; and whether the market for broadcast programmes is functioning to the benefit of the people whom the Broadcasting Act 2003 refers to as both citizens and consumers. This combination, which Ofcom occasionally marries into a single term 'citizen-consumer', recognises the complexity of the activity of regulation. As broadcasting diversifies, the trend in regulation is towards less intervention by regulatory bodies and more regulation by market forces. However tempting this might seem to some politicians and even broadcasters, it ignores the social status of broadcasting as a basic provider of the information needed to make society and markets function efficiently.»

How do you work the remote control?

Television has become the centre of a complicated mesh of technological decisions, which many people find confusing. Innovations have been driven by two desires: the desire for increased choice in programming and the desire for better picture and sound quality. Sometimes, as with digital broadcasting, the two come together; more often, they are simply parallel developments. There are various boxes which will give increased choice to any kind of television, and screens that will offer high-definition images and surround-sound effects.

The result is that most televisions are now surrounded by an archipelago of wires, boxes and remote controls. There are digital decoders, DVD and VHS players and stereo speakers; there are PVR boxes that scoop up hundreds of programmes to choose from; there are SCART and co-axial cables and cable and satellite cables. Everything has its own remote control. There are even more boxes that eliminate the need for some of the cables; glowing green lights and blinking red ones, all using up energy because most of them demand that they are left on permanently,

» Q45

sometimes with power-hungry voltage adaptors.» There are choices to be made between plasma and LED screens; widescreen and high-definition screens and home cinema projection systems. There are competing formats to replace DVDs, competing offerings for subscription services. There are tantalising possibilities of TV over the Internet, TV on mobile phones, TV on portable devices like iPods. For a casual and everyday medium, it is surprising how TV has increasingly ensnarled itself in complications. TV is now as entangled in decisions as the average domestic TV is entangled in wires. The maturing of the medium is experienced by many users as an unnecessary complication which stands between them and their viewing.

This has followed a period of technical simplicity in which the increasing reliability of TV technology combined with a relatively slow incremental rate of innovation, mainly around providing additional channels. Until the spread of transistor technology in the 1970s, TV sets had been relatively unreliable if not dangerous, involving fragile valves running at high voltages. This made TV sets 'the most dangerous piece of technology ever put in the hands of consumers', as I was once told by a salesman. A whole industry of TV repair grew up around this in the 1950s and 1960s, with the TV repair man being a familiar domestic caller, and the subject of the same kind of innuendo as the milkman.[101] The TV repair man is now a vanished profession, perhaps the first vanished profession of the electronic age.

The simplicity and reliability of TV technology from the 1970s meant that, once installed, problems were rare as long as the licence fee and satellite subscription were paid on time. The only problem was the VCR (video cassette recorder), which arrived in the late 1970s and was becoming widespread by the early 1980s. Everyone could see the usefulness of its timeshifting and programme-preservation capabilities. But it came with a technological challenge: how to programme it to record in advance. In many households, this valuable feature remained underused because of the complicated menus of options involved in what would seem to be the simple task of setting time, date and channel.

The newer generation of VCRs tried to dispense with this by introducing number codes for scheduled programmes. However, 'only the children know how to programme the VCR' became a standard remark for many years, reflecting a level of frustration rather than technophobia. Often manuals were written in a form that many found difficult to understand, perhaps because of bad translation, perhaps because they were drafted with little empathy with the eventual users, or even regard for elementary logic. As Ann Gray discovered in her research,[102] these technologies also interacted with family dynamics in a very unfortunate way. Men tended to take control of the remote control, sometimes grabbing it from the hands of women and children. Women, who were adept at programming washing machines (with their complex series of choices expressed through icons), were discouraged from learning the icons and routines of VCRs.

New TV technologies bring problems of accessibility for those who are old, infirm or otherwise challenged, and for them and many more, the VCR experience was a depressing experience. At least it did not affect the accessibility of TV itself, but only the extra possibility of timeshift viewing. But among the range of new technological possibilities there are also additions to the basic TV service. So the transition to digital broadcasting universalises the problem of understanding menus of choices and adapting to new formats. Digital broadcasting replaces the increasing fuzziness of a failing analogue signal with a simple 'either it works or it doesn't' binary. The proliferation of technologies brings an increased potential for failing interfaces as one manufacturer's software subtly misunderstands another's. Every new item comes with its own design of menu, relating to its own design of remote control, and its own version of icons. Although standardisation of such design is taking place, and manufacturers are understandably eager to research 'intuitive interfaces', it is a slow process. This increased complication appeals to a more male interest in gadgets at the expense of a more general interest in programmes and content. Many users are frustrated that they have to make a voyage of exploration of a piece of technology when they really want a voyage of exploration of TV programmes.

All of these innovations aim to make TV more pliable and adaptable. Always a medium that was eager to please, TV is now facing new requirements from sections of its audience. Some want images and sounds that they can manipulate. Some want TV that is always available, wherever they are. Some want TV to act as a background to everyday life. Some want TV that provides an intense, compelling experience of viewing. Some want what's already there but at a time that suits their particular lifestyle rather than the generalised pattern of the schedule. Some want a particular range of programmes.

To this seemingly endless list of requirements, the TV industry has one answer: choice. Choices of what to watch, where to watch, when to watch, how to adjust its images and sounds, now abound, and have multiplied in a decade. Even the size and shape of a TV picture is now in flux, both in production and at home. Some programmes are produced in widescreen, others not. They are seen on screens where viewers can change the aspect ratio if they want, squeezing widescreen into a standard format or stretching standard format images to widescreen. In many homes, it is likely that some default setting somewhere on the menu may well be dictating such alterations anyway.

This proliferation of technologies allows many people to customise their equipment to suit the particular way that they use TV. For an industry, and a public, who have been used to a 'one size fits all' model of transmission, this is a considerable change, and adaptation is proving difficult. TV is now a matter of menus that branch off into sub-menus. Finding something decent to watch is getting more difficult as the number of available channels increases. All kinds of helpful devices have been created. The Electronic Programme Guide (EPG) lists on-screen what's showing on all the channels or classifies by genre of programme; recording devices like TiVO or SkyPlus that can store what they judge, from your previous viewing, you might want to watch. Handy printed programme guides fall out of almost all the weekend newspapers, complete with preview comments and picks of the day. Every commercial break seems to contain trails for other offerings on the same channel or other members of its 'family', and end credits are an opportunity for announcers to recommend what's coming up. Yet many households confine their viewing to around a dozen channels.[103]

In the UK, research is demonstrating how the main terrestrial channels maintain their share of the audience by launching a 'family' of spin-off channels.[104]**»** The trusted nature of brands along with the existing market power of the main broadcasters**»** appears to be a powerful force in informing viewer choice. *Broadcast* magazine commissioned research that showed this would be a long-term trend, as 'much of the decline of the main terrestrial channels will be offset by the growth of channels such as ITV2, BBC3 and E4.'[105]

Q44 How do you work the remote control?

Currently, TV offers both choices of technologies and choices enabled by those technologies. This proliferation of choice has developed after a period of technological transparency, when viewers had direct and simple access to programmes. Technological sophistication endangers the easy universality that this transparency gave to TV. Two groups may be disadvantaged by the loss of this transparency: people who watch very little TV and viewers who, for whatever reason, have difficulty in adapting to new technologies. They may give up TV completely, which will be a particular problem for those elderly who find in TV a way of remaining connected with the wider world as their physical horizons shrink. This would reduce the universality of broadcast TV, which is one of its social strengths. However, emerging research is beginning to demonstrate a strong attachment to the communal phenomenon of the core terrestrial channels.

Is TV bad for the environment?

TV sets are hazardous waste according to the Department for Environment (DEFRA)'s 2005 Hazardous Waste Regulations. This is hardly surprising since the average glass cathode ray tube TV contains between four and eight pounds of lead, along with a series of chemicals which accumulate in the bodies of humans and other mammals, including brominated fire retardants. In the UK, households dispose of old TVs in substantial numbers, and few are refurbished for resale. The Industry Council for Electronic Equipment Recycling estimated that the weight of glass in waste TVs will increase over time from 69,000 tonnes in 2002 to some 90,000 tonnes by 2012,[106] since more glass is used in more recent tubes. The rapid transition to flat-screen TVs with LCD or plasma screens is likely to increase the number of glass tube sets that households want to get rid of. The DEFRA regulations put a duty of care on households to dispose of unwanted TVs responsibly, but many still end up in landfill.

The TV sets disposed of in 2002 also contained an estimated 24,883 tonnes of plastic. Recycling the backs of TV sets presents particular problems since 'the presence of halogenated flame retardants can cause health and safety problems during some recycling processes because toxic fumes are released if extrusion is carried out at high temperatures.'[107] The risk with these substances is not confined to the disposal process; they also leach out of TV set casings during their use. WWF has identified the presence of brominated fire retardants in the bodies of even young people, with the most likely sources being carpets, sofas, TV sets and computers. TV sets and computers are a particularly problematic source as they tend to warm the plastic, so increasing the trace emissions of this substance. The long-term effects of brominated fire retardants are unknown. 'The chemistry and environmental behaviour of BFRs can be compared with that of PCBs. They are just as persistent and some are highly bioaccumulative, although little is yet known about their toxicity.'[108] At least two TV manufacturers (Samsung and Bang & Olufsen) are committed to phasing them out.

TV sets are an environmental problem like every other large item of electronic equipment. In addition, they are hungry in their power consumption in everyday use, and look set to increase that power consumption. Flat-screen TVs consume more power than cathode ray tubes. According to the Energy Saving Trust, the average power supply for a glass tube TV is 90 watts, but for a plasma screen it is 400 watts.[109] TV sets consume forty per cent of all the power used by domestic electronics.[110] TV equipment has long been manufactured so that 'switching off' does not stop power consumption. Instead, TVs and video cassette recorders (VCRs) are programmed to go into standby mode, generating an absolute waste of power which is quite extraordinary. The UK government estimates that eight per cent of all electricity used in homes was wasted in this way in 2004, and 'the trend is rising.'[111] In the UK, TV sets left on standby waste £88m worth of energy and 480,000 tonnes of CO2, and VCRs are even more profligate, wasting £175m worth of energy and 960,000 tonnes of CO2.[112] Sony's own website calculates that this represents 68.7 per cent of the CO2 emissions involved in the manufacture and use of a VCR, against 15.4 per cent generated by their actual usage. The proportions for TV sets are quite different. TV sets on standby generate just 3.2 per cent of their CO2 emissions, and usage produces 81.8 per cent.[113] Sony claims to be making efforts to reduce this level of power consumption, and the UK government is attempting to get the provision of a default standby mode eliminated.

The phasing out of VCR as a recording and replay technology is taking place relatively fast in the UK, so this should reduce the emissions from that source progressively. However, as is the way in these matters, when one energy-profligate source is disappearing, another appears. The new problem is the set-top boxes which are becoming a **》** 044 standard feature of TV homes.**》** These boxes provide digital signals to the millions of analogue TV screens of all kinds, and often act as PVRs (personal video recorders) as well. They are set up to be always on, partly so that they can be ready to receive software updates. The UK government is formally committed to reducing the power consumption of such devices, according to the Energy Saving Trust, which it partly funds.[114] However, the government is also committed to converting all TV transmission to digital by 2012, so is equally concerned that the price of such devices should remain low. Any additional functions would increase their price. So it is unlikely that digital set-top boxes will be given the intelligent update checker provided with digital tuners built into those plasma sets which can be turned off. According to one journalist, 'Using current technology, the change to digital would result in a Europe-wide electricity requirement of 60 terra-watt-hours of electric energy just to power digital boxes (equivalent to the electricity consumption of Denmark), releasing 24 million tones of extra CO2.'[115]

So TV is bad for the environment. Standby and always-on devices are the worst culprits, since they waste substantial amounts of power, which Friends of the Earth estimates to be the equivalent of the output of one 1,000-megawatt nuclear power station.[116] The disposal of glass tube sets in large numbers in the coming years will generate substantial lead waste, and the continuing presence of potentially harmful brominated fire retardants is a little-understood potential biological hazard for the future. TV viewers can make a substantial contribution to reducing two of these problems. They can reduce power waste by turning off equipment rather than leaving it on standby, including set-top boxes, most of which do provide a menu option for a manual search for updates. Unwanted TV sets can be sent for recycling, and there is already a theoretical requirement on their owners to dispose of them through the specialised facilities of local waste sites. However, it is odd that such advice does not appear on UK TV itself, even at the end of environmentally aware wildlife programmes like the BBC's *Planet Earth*.

Will downloading replace broadcasting?

If you can access programmes from the Internet at DVD standard, does broadcasting have any future? One answer has it that it doesn't matter how you access something, it is still the content that is king. However, the kind of content that people tend to access depends to a considerable degree on the form of access. Just as the standard format of a series of distinct yet similar episodes is a creation, more or less, of broadcasting, so Internet downloading may begin to produce forms of content of its own. Downloaded content may well be less time-dependent than broadcast content. Downloading depends on a greater level of decision than accessing a scheduled broadcast from one channel rather than another. Broadcasting carries an insistence ('watch now: this is on now, and something else will be on later'). Downloading has no such insistence, implying a greater degree of commitment from the consumer to the particular item being downloaded, but no particular outside pressure to consume.

Broadcasting's insistence has depended on the idea that you have to watch it now or you'll miss it. This, at least until the video recorder, was a drawback with broadcasting, especially for people with something else to do. The 'watch it now' insistence of a particular broadcast depends on the currency of the programme concerned, the way that it fits into the wider patterns and preoccupations of life. Classically this was carried out by scheduling, trying to fit programmes to the predicted mood of the particular moments in which they are broadcast. In the era of multiple channels, successful programmes increasingly need to achieve a general cultural currency as well. They refer to current events and become a topic of conversation in themselves.**»**

» Q33

TV series like *The X Factor* or *The Apprentice*, *Desperate Housewives* or *Sex and the City*, *What Not to Wear* or *Who Do You Think You Are?* become temporary phenomena. The characters or presenters are featured in journalism of various kinds; broadcasters and fans alike create websites;

spin-off programming emerges; all and any kind of merchandise and product marketing connections appear in shops. The series enters into the life cycle of the TV success. Initially, the series is novel and remarkable. It gradually becomes compelling and fascinating and then, after perhaps a couple of years, familiar and reassuring. Eventually it becomes worn out, even after repeated injections of new characters and/or format twists. Then it is taken off,» only to reappear in the guise of nostalgia. This pattern can be seen in series as different as the gardening makeover show *Ground Force*, sitcoms like *I Love Lucy* from the 1950s or *Friends* from the 1990s; dramas like *The Rockford Files*, *Dynasty* or *Peak Practice*. The process often takes a decade or longer with an enduring success, but it is still a temporary time-tied phenomenon. Series like *Friends* or *Dynasty* seem to define their times, not least because they successfully embody particular preoccupations of those times along with their dubious clothes and hairstyles.»

All of this is tied into a very particular time frame, which is key to broadcasting: the time period of the week. Broadcast TV increasingly consists of series of weekly episodes. The single programme is a rarity, remarked as a 'special' where once it was the typical form of TV. Each episode of a series has a week's presence, a currency that is increasingly reflected in the scheduling of broadcasts across different and linked channels. Tonight's episode has become the current episode, available across the week in different slots on the different channels in the broadcaster's group. After a week's exposure, another episode takes its place, moving the story along in the gradual pace that seems a part of TV's currency. Incidents happen each week, but the main dilemmas of the characters continue to uncoil for months and even years. The gradual evolution of Sipowitz in *NYPD Blue* is an outstanding case. He was initially a foul-tempered sociopath whose obscure sense of justice led him to break the rules rather too often. After thirteen years, he closed the series by becoming station captain, having endured a stormy courtship and the loss of his wife, single parenting and cancer and more work partners than anyone can easily remember. He even had to deal with the aftermath of 9/11. From the start, the series had signalled that the exploration of the troubled man behind the gruff exterior would be one of its aims.

A series like *NYPD Blue* becomes part of the pattern of everyday life, gathering different kinds of viewers from the devoted to those who watch just occasionally to see how the characters are getting on (or whether they are still there at all). This is the viewing pattern of the long period of familiarity enjoyed by many successes, and it extends beyond formats to presenters and even genres. This pattern depends on the limited currency of each episode, creating a kind of extended and common present in a particular broadcast market. It can have its odd effects, as when UK audiences suddenly seem to have a crop of Christmases in March when viewing imported American series like *ER*.

Will the multiplication of channels and the development of entirely new means of delivery (downloads to Personal Media Devices; mobile-phone viewing etc) reduce the effectiveness of such forms? The available evidence seems to show that it will not. Developments include an increase in the broadcast form of temporary presence, along with other new forms. Some popular downloads are in effect variants of broadcasting, depending on a currency of nowness. Some are even streams rather than downloads, so it has to be watched when sent from the host site, which gives them a few more of the attributes of a broadcast.

In this sense, there is no difference between a celebrity-based TV show and a celebrity-based download of stars having sex, except that TV broadcasting is subject to editorial controls which prevent the latter material from

» 043

being shown.» Neither is there much difference between 'real' TV commercials and the popular downloads of spoof commercials like the Trojan Olympics campaign of naked athletes converting real sports events into awkward sex acts. These looked like TV commercials (and indeed were taken as such by many outside the UK) but were available only as downloads whose availability was advertised by so-called viral marketing: people emailing links to their contacts followed by archly 'knowing' mentions in the press. This is the Internet behaving like a broadcast medium, where what is accessed depends on its public currency just like a broadcast programme. Underlying this is a desire on the part of the individual to be part of something that is happening.

As well as that desire, people also want to be different and distinctive, to have their own interests. This personal rather than public currency is better served by the library function that can be provided by the Internet, rather than the exclusively live streaming form of broadcasting. The web is far better suited to on-demand provision: it waits there until the moment you want it. The web provides an increasing access to historical TV material which often has a specialised, research interest rather than a continuing use as entertainment.» Broadcasting is an on-supply form, depending on its contemporary relevance for its temporary success. Web material is likely to display fewer of these temporarily meaningful or relevant aspects of broadcasting.

The web will, therefore, create different forms. These are more likely to emerge from the peer-to-peer (interpersonal) communication aspects of the web than they are from centralised content-creating companies. The web is driven by searching and finding; TV is driven by provision from trusted sources. TV channels have a strong editorial identity that brands their content.» The brands and market power of the existing broadcasters seems to be giving them significant advantages even against other broadcast competitors in the multichannel TV environment.» TV is a centralised content-creating industry, and the web behaves in a very different way. The leading edge of the TV industry is already searching through web content for ideas, transferring material and talent to a general audience. This will become a more common feature of the future: TV channels will act as publishers for material that has found specific appeal on the web, bringing it to the attention of viewers who have not searched for and found it. Broadcasting and the web therefore have complementary and interdependent but rather different roles.

) Q35

) Q37

) Q44

Q46 Will downloading replace broadcasting?

Notes

1. 'Original production ("originations" or "originated output") includes all output excluding repeats and programmes acquired from other broadcasters. In 2005, 131,066 hours were originated, with the multichannels accounting for 65% of the total (85,796 hours). The five main channels continued to play a role as the 'engine' of originations, making a substantial 16% contribution (20,752 hours) in contrast to their broadcasting just 6% of total hours. A further 11% came from the BBC's digital channels, who together commissioned 14,013 hours in 2005. Nations and regions made up the remaining 8% or 10,505 hours.' Ofcom, *The Communications Market 2006*, 10 August 2006, p. 208, available at: http://www.ofcom.org.uk/research/cm/cm06/. According to table 4.24, the total of hours originated by the five terrestrial channels was 45,270 (with multichannels providing 85,796); table 4.25 shows that their total investment was £2,950 million to the multichannels' £1,742 million.

2. '16–24 year olds watch substantially less television than older people and their viewing is declining at a faster rate, down by over one and a half hours, to 18 hours and 18 minutes per week, over the past four years (against a 1% rise for the adult population). In addition, their exposure to television is declining; just 84% watched at least an average of 15 consecutive minutes per week in June 2006, whereas the "all individuals" figure was 92%" Ofcom, ibid, p. 41.

3. This much older strain of complaint about the nature of modern culture, particularly mass culture, can be found in the works of the Frankfurt School (particularly Theodor Adorno) and the poet/critic Matthew Arnold.

4. Silverstone, Roger (2007), p. 166.

5. The effect of these new sources of news is to reduce the audience for the traditional news bulletins at key moments in the evening, rather than to erode the importance of TV as a news source. see Ofcom, The Communications Market 2006, 10 August 2006, p. 273.

6. Ibid., p. 269.

7. See for instance the film *Outfoxed* (2006), directed by Robert Greenwald.

8. 'In this idea originated the plan of the "Lyrical Ballads"; in which it was agreed, that my endeavours should be directed to persons and characters supernatural, or at least romantic, yet so as to transfer from our inward nature a human interest and a semblance of truth sufficient to procure for these shadows of imagination that willing suspension of disbelief for the moment, which constitutes poetic faith.' Samuel Taylor Coleridge, *Biographia Literaria*, 1817, Chapter XIV.

9. See Winston, Brian (2000).

10. See Ellis, John (2005b)

11. *The Connection*, ITV, 15 October 1998, 22.40

12. See Turnock, Rob (2007).

13. According to the Office of National Statistics, the number of households in the UK in 2002 was 25,026,000. The source for the number of TV sets and the proportion watching each week is BARB, and for the distribution of those sets around the home, Ofcom Report 2004, table 9. Table 22 of this same report specifies that in homes with analogue TVs, they watched 3.4 hours per day, and in digital homes 3.8 hours a day.

14. Scannell, Paddy (2000).

15. This is not actually true, as the general level of 'visual literacy' has increased during the half century of mass TV. Programmes can assume a much greater level of sophistication in their audiences.

16. Estimate quoted in Joe Garner, *Stay Tuned* (Kansas City: Andrews McMeal, 2002), p. 81.

17. Liebes, Tamar and Elihu Katz (1993)

18. IPPR report, December 2006.

19. Television practice in the UK requires that a signed 'consent form' exists for all participants in a programme. Such forms are often offered for signature before the filming begins, and the wary will put off signing them until afterwards. However, in some cases like investigative filming, the requirement for a consent form is waived for obvious reasons.

20. See http://www.courttv.com/archive/verdicts/schmitz.html, which provides notes from Schmitz's first trial. He was eventually convicted at a second trial on 26 August 1999 as the first trial was deficient in its procedures. The programme itself, being pre-recorded, was never transmitted. *The Jenny Jones Show*, first aired in 1991, continued until 2003 when it was cancelled.

21. Source: Ofcom, *The Communications Market 2004: Television*, Appendix tables 1, 5, 6.

22. See Collett, Peter and Roger Lamb (1986), and B. Gunter, A. Furnham and Z. Lineton (1995)

23. 'How People Use® Primetime TV 2004 Knowledge Networks'. Quote from press release on their website www.knowledgenetworks.com, dated 1 December 2004.

24. Kaiser Family Foundation, 'Generation M: Media in the Lives of 8–18 Year-Olds', Washington DC, 2005.

25. Frank B. Hu et al., 'Television Watching and Other Sedentary Behaviors in Relation to Risk of Obesity and Type 2 Diabetes Mellitus in Women', *Journal of the American Medical Association*, 2003, no. 289: 1785–1791.

26. http://www.holistic-online.com/Remedies/weight/weight_risk-factors-and-causes-of-obesity.htm.

27. See Livingstone, Sonia and Moira Bovill (2001)

28. 'Ironically, Jade's habit of stumbling over words was once the most endearing thing about her. Confusing "Picasso" with "Pistaccio" was a genuine and loveable mistake.' *Heat*, 27 January 2007, p. 16.

29. *The Christian O'Connell Breakfast Show*, on Xfm from 2003 then on Virgin Radio from 2006.

30. According to BARB figures at the point of the invasion of Iraq

Notes

in the week of 22 March 2003, around fifty-one per cent of multichannel viewers watched a rolling news channel for three minutes or more. By the first week in May, this figure had reduced to its normal level of around eleven per cent. Source: J. Sanch and J. Glover, *Conflict Around the Clock* (Ofcom/ITC, 2004), p. 18.

31.   See Peters, John Durham (2000) and (1999)

32.   Katherine Flett, *The Observer*, 12 September 2004.

33.   Tom Junod, 'The Falling Man', *Esquire*, September 2003, Volume 140, Issue 3.

34.   See Ellis, John (2000).

35.   See Scannell (2005), p. 578.

36.   *USA Today*, 2 September 2002.

37.   Junod, op.cit.

38.   There is an 11-minute film short with the same title also related to 9/11 directed by Kevin Akerman.

39.   Scannell (2005), p. 573.

40.   *Oxford Dictionary of Modern Quotations*.

41.   These also include 'chugging' (i.e. charity mugging) approaches in the street, and multiple mailings. Charity donation itself is one way, rather than the only way, of expressing concern and compassion; other means might be joining political demonstrations or campaign groups. But see also Boltanski (1999).

42.   Fiske, John and John Hartley (1978)

43.   See Gledhill, Christine (1987); Rowe, Kathleen (1995).

44.   Johnson-Smith, Jan (2004).

45.   BBC Drama brochure for 1997–1998, quoted Jack Kibble-White, http://www.offthetelly.co.uk/drama/cops.htm.

46.   Gareth Neame, BBC Head of Independent Commissioning until 2005, http://www.bbc.co.uk/pressoffice/pressreleases/stories/2002/07_july/03/trust.shtml.

47.   http://www.bbc.co.uk/pressoffice/pressreleases/stories/2002/10_october/29/servants.shtml.

48.   David Edgar, 'What Are we Telling the Nation', *London Review of Books*, 7 July 2005, vol. 27, n. 13.

49.   *NYPD Blue* ended in March 2005 after twelve seasons totalling 261 episodes, plus a couple of specials.

50.   'Guns n Rosaries' first aired on ABC in the USA on 10 May 1994.

51.   'A PR [Puerto Rican] cop kills a brother and what am I supposed to do?' as one Latino witness succinctly puts it.

52.   Butler, Jeremy (2001)

53.   'Soap Box or Soft Soap: Audience Attitudes to the British Soap Opera', Broadcasting Standards Commission report, August 2002.

54.   Ibid. pp. 24–5.

55.   This does not make it the longest-running soap in US TV, however. The record is held by *The Guiding Light*, which began on radio in January 1937 and was still searching for an ending on CBS in 2007.

56.   Source: Tim Horan, executive vice-president of the production company Amedia, speaking at TVMasnovelas 2006, Madrid,

October 2006, reported at http://www.onlytelenovelas.com/Only_8/11.php.

57. This was the case for Stephen Frear's ITV drama *The Queen* (2006), but was not for his previous dramatisation of recent political events for Channel 4, *The Deal* (2003).

58. Lury, Karen (2005) p. 61.

59. I prefer the term 'connoisseur' to 'fan', as the term 'fan' tends to carry negative connotations, indicating someone whose expertise is regarded as trivial.

60. See Annette Hill's fascinating interviews in *Reality TV* (2005).

61. Ibid. p. 133.

62. See Richard Mabey, *Selected Writings 1974–1999* (London: Chatto and Windus, 1999), pp. 128–35.

63. For those without Internet access, the amounts were proportionately greater: USA 16.8 hours, Germany 22.9 hours; Japan 26.3 hours. Source: http://www.international.ucla.edu/article.asp?parentid=7488.

64. Report by Chris Curtis, *Broadcast*, 5 October 2006.

65. From http://www.bbc.co.uk/cult/classic/titles/whydontyou.shtml, consulted November 2005.

66. The estimated figure is for 31 March 2004. See: http://www.bbccharterreview.org.uk/pdf_documents/040716BBC_Funding_Facts_and_Figures.pdf.

67. Eleanor Bailey, *The Observer*, 13 July 2003.

68. Claire Phipps, 'Dear Claire', *The Guardian*, 6 January 2005.

69. This process is discussed at the 'Jump the Shark' website, http://www.jumptheshark.com/, which describes itself as 'documenting the moment when shows go downhill'.

70. See Robert Hinshelwood, *A Dictionary of Kleinian Thought* (Free Association Books 1993).

71. Sources: hours from *Broadcast*, 22 July 2005, p. 2; proportions from 'The Communications Market 2005', Ofcom, 2005, p. 227.

72. For instance, on Saturday 16 July 2005 at 5.45pm, *Only Fools and Horses* had 3.2 million viewers, a twenty-eight per cent share of the viewing audience. *Broadcast*, 22 July 2005).

73. See Ellis, John (2000).

74. Caldwell, John T. (1995).

75. This solid and unpretentious primetime series has so far produced more than 250 episodes since it first aired in April 1992 at the rate of up to twenty-five a year. This rivals long-running American successes like *NYPD Blue*. Its cosy world of police business in a Yorkshire town and surrounding area still attracts audiences of up to ten million for ITV1.

76. Two shillings and six pence, now the equivalent of 12.5 pence, but, between 1964 and 1967, it would buy five copies of the BBC listings magazine *Radio Times*.

77. Hutcheon, Linda (2000) p. 193

78. Though it appears that the producers of Hollywood films assume the rules of baseball to be universally known, though many Europeans do not know them.

79. See Bourdieu, Pierre (1993).

80. Speech to RTS London Conference, *Television*, October 2006, p. 9.

Notes

81. Earlier in the series' long run, it had used its monopoly status to experiment in the kinds of people featured: a famous over-65s edition, a pioneering gay edition and so on.

82. BARB website, January 2007: 25.9 million households; 25.3million with TV sets: http://www.barb.co.uk/TVFACTS. cfm?fullstory=true&includepage=ownership&flag=tvfacts.

83. 'Comment – Show some appreciation', *Broadcast*, 16 January 2004.

84. Speech given by Jane Root, Controller of BBC Two, speaking to the Royal Television Society at BAFTA, Piccadilly, London W1, Tuesday 10 February 2004, *Television* vol. 41, n. 3, March 2004.

85. BBC, 'Building Public Value: Renewing the BBC for a Digital World' (2004), pp. 83–8.

86. See http://www.opendemocracy.net/debates/article.jsp?id=8&debate Id=38&articleId=57.

87. Skillset, 'Survey of the Audio Visual Industries' Workforce' (2005), p. 35.

88. Ibid. p. 96.

89. Ibid. p. 28.

90. The working population of the UK is around thirty million according to the Office of National Statistics.

91. The Office of National Statistics lists 44,000 people employed in the category of 'broadcasting associated professionals' in the quarter April–June 2006.

92. The working population being 150 million according to the Department of Labor's seasonally adjusted figures.

93. Dominic Toto, 'Job Growth in Television: Cable versus Broadcast, 1958–1999', *Monthly Labor Review*, August 2000, p. 4.

94. Quarterly estimates of 'All in Employment', April–June 2006.

95. Skillset, 'Getting In', http://www.skillset.org/careers/.

96. See http://www.bbc.co.uk/guidelines/editorialguidelines/edguide/.

97. See http://www.bbc.co.uk/guidelines/editorialguidelines/edguide/war/editorialprinci.shtml.

98. Ofcom, 'Broadcasting Code', p. 2.

99. Both were Labour-supporting millionaires (worth at least £40 million and £10 million respectively).

100. Milne was summarily sacked some two years later over another controversial programme about government, the *Secret Society* series.

101. Milkmen were the butt of jokes about their relations with women who were at home during the day

102. Grey, Ann (1992).

103. See for instance: Manish Bhatia, 'TV Viewing in Internet Homes', Nielsen Media Research, May 1999, p. 1: 'By 1998, the average TV home was able to receive 57 channels. While the number of channels available in the TV home continues to grow, the number of channels actually viewed has not grown beyond 13. (The term 'viewed' is defined as 10 or more continuous minutes per channel.)'

104. 'However, in some ways, the five mainstream channels taken together with their spinoffs have benefited more than new operators from the growth in multichannel television;

viewing share of their spin-off channels rose from 3% to 9% in multichannel homes between 2001 and 2005, more than offsetting the 1.2 percentage point drop in share of the parent channels. The share of 'non-terrestrial' new channels meanwhile fell from 39% to 34% in multichannel homes, as audiences grew but fragmented.' Ofcom, 'Communications Market 2006', 10 August 2006, p. 21.

105. *Broadcast*, 8 December 2006, p. 1; see also 15 December 2006, p. 19.
106. Materials Recovery From Waste Cathode Ray Tubes (CRTs), Waste & Resources Action Programme, 2004, p. 13.
107. Ibid. p. 18.
108. WWF Report.
109. Energy Saving Trust, 'Energy and Waste in an Age of Excess', 26 October 2005.
110. Energy Saving Trust, 'Rise of the Machines', 2006, p. 34.
111. 'The Energy Challenge', DTI Cmnd 6887, July 2006, p. 43.
112. 'Energy and Waste', op cit.
113. See http://www.sony.net/SonyInfo/Environment/environment/communication/ecoplaza/ecolife/index.html.
114. 'Rise of Machines', op cit. p.16.
115. Lucy Siegle, *The Observer*, 10 September 2006.
116. Friends of the Earth press release, 'Energy review must pave way for clean and safe energy', 29 November 2005.

Where can I find out more?

Abercrombie, Nicholas, and Brian Longhurst (1998) *Diffused Audience: Sociological Theory and Audience Research* (London: Sage)

Allen, Robert (ed.) (1998), *To Be Continued: Soap Opera around the World* (London: Routledge)

Anderson, Christopher (1994) *Hollywood TV: The Studio System in the Fifties* (University of Texas Press)

Ang, Ien (1991), *Desperately Seeking the Audience* (London: Routledge)

———— (1986)*Watching Dallas: Soap Opera and the Melodramatic Imagination* (London: Routledge)

Barker, C. (1997), *Global Television: An Introduction* (Oxford: Blackwell)

Barker, Martin, and Julian Petley (eds.) (2001), *Ill Effects: The Media Violence Debate* (London: Routledge)

Bignell, Jonathan (2003), *An Introduction to Television Studies* (London: Routledge)

Bird, S. Elizabeth (2003), *The Audience in Everyday Life: Living in a Media World* (London: Routledge)

Boltanski, Luc (1999), *Distant Suffering: Morality, Media and Politics* (Cambridge: Cambridge University Press)

Bonner, Frances (2002), *Ordinary Television* (London: Sage)

Bourdieu, Pierre (1986), *Distinction: A Social Critique of the Judgement of Taste* (London: Routledge)

———— (1993), *The Field of Cultural Production* (Cambridge: Polity Press)

Bourdon, Jerome (2003), 'Live Television Is Still Alive: On Television as an Unfulfilled Promise', in A. Hill and R. Allen (eds.), *The Television Studies Reader* (London: Routledge)

Boyle, Raymond, and Richard Haynes (2004), *Football in the New Media Age* (London: Routledge)

Bruzzi, Stella (2000), *New Documentary: A Critical Introduction* (London: Routledge)

Burke, David (ed.) (1999), *Spy TV: Just Who Is the Digital TV Revolution Overthrowing?* (Brighton: Slab-O-Concrete Publications)

Burke, David, and Jean Lotus (1998), *Get a Life! The Little Red Book of the White Dot* (London: Bloomsbury)

Butler, Jeremy (2002), *Television: Critical Methods and Applications* (New Jersey: Lawrence Erlbaum Associates)

———— (2001) 'VR in the ER: ER's use of e-media', *Screen Winter 2001*, pp.313–31

Caldwell, John T. (1995), *Televisuality: Style, Crisis and Authority in American Television* (New Jersey: Rutgers University Press)

Casey, Benadette, Neil Casey, Ben Calvert, Liam French and Justin Lewis (2002), *Television Studies: The Key Concepts* (London: Routledge)

Caughie, John (2002), *Television Drama: Realism, Modernism and British Culture* (Oxford: Oxford University Press)

Chion, Michel (1994), *Audio-Vision: Sound on Screen* (New York: Columbia University Press)

Collett, Peter, and Roger Lamb (1986),*Watching People Watching Television* (London: Independent Broadcasting Authority)

Corner, John (1999), *Critical Ideas in Television Studies* (Oxford: Oxford

University Press)

—— (1996), *The Art of Record: A Critical Introduction to Documentary* (Manchester: Manchester University Press)

Corner, John, and Alan Rosenthal (eds.) (2005), *New Challenges in Documentary* (Manchester: Manchester University Press)

Cottle, Simon (2003), *News, Public Relations and Power* (London: Sage)

—— (ed.) (2003b) *Media Organisations and Production* (London: Sage)

Couldry, Nick (2000), *The Place of Media Power: Pilgrims and Witnesses of the Media Age* (London: Routledge)

Creeber, Glen (2001), *The Television Genre Book* (London: British Film Institute)

Dahlgren, Peter (1995), *Television and the Public Sphere: Citizenship, Democracy and the Media* (London: Sage)

Dayan, Daniel (1998), 'Particularist Media and Diasporic Communications', in T. Liebes and J. Curran (eds.), *Media Ritual and Identity* (London: Routledge), pp. 103–13

Dayan, Daniel and Elihu Katz (1992), *Media Events: The Live Broadcasting of History* (Massachusetts: Harvard University Press)

Dovey, Jon (2000), *Freakshow: First Person Media and Factual Television* (London: Pluto Press)

Ellis, John (2007) 'Immanent Reading versus Textual Historicism', in H. Wheatley (ed.), *Re-Viewing Television History* (London: I.B.Tauris)

—— (2005a), 'Importance, Significance, Cost And Value: Is An ITV Canon Possible?', in C. Johnson and R. Turnock (eds.), *ITV Cultures: Fifty Years of Commercial Television* (Open University Press), pp. 36–56

—— (2005b), 'Documentary and Truth on Television: The Crisis of 1999', in J. Corner and A. Rosenthal (eds.) (2005), pp.342–60.

—— (2003), 'Television Production', in R. Allen and A. Hill (eds.), *The Television Studies Reader* (London: Routledge), pp. 275–92

—— (2002), 'A Minister is About to Resign: On the Interpretation of Television Footage', in A. Jerslev (ed.), *Realism and 'Reality' in Film and Media* (University of Copenhagen Press), pp. 193–210

—— (2000), *Seeing Things: Television in the Age of Uncertainty* (London: I.B.Tauris)

—— (1982), *Visible Fictions: Cinema, Television, Video* (London: Routledge)

Fiske, John and John Hartley (1978), *Reading Television* (London: Methuen)

Gauntlett, David and Annette Hill (1999), *TV Living: Television, Culture and Everyday Life* (London: Routledge)

Geraghty, Christine (1991), *Women and Soap Opera* (Cambridge: Polity)

Geraghty, Christine, and David Lusted (1998), *The Television Studies Book* (London: Edward Arnold)

Gitlin, Todd (1994), *Inside Prime Time* (revised edition, London: Routledge)

Gledhill, Christine (ed.) (1987), *Home Is Where the Heart Is: Studies in Melodrama and Women's Film* (London: British Film Institute)

Gray, Ann (1992), *Video Playtime: The Gendering of a Leisure Technology* (London: Routledge)

Gripsrud, Jostein (2002), *Understanding Media Culture* (London: Hodder Arnold)

Where can I find out more?

———— (1995), *The 'Dynasty' Years: Hollywood Television and Critical Media Studies* (London: Routledge)

———— (ed.) (1999) *Television and Common Knowledge* (London: Routledge)

Gunter, B., A. Furnham and Z. Lineton (1995), 'Watching people watching television', *Journal of Educational Television*, 21(3), pp.165–91

Hartley, John (1999), *The Uses of Television* (Routledge, London)

Hill, Annette (2005), *Reality TV: Audiences and Popular Factual Television* (London: Routledge)

Hobsbawm, Eric (1995), *The Age of Extremes: The Short Twentieth Century* (London: Abacus)

Holmes, Su, and Deborah Jermyn (eds.) (2003), *Understanding Reality Television* (London: Routledge)

Hutcheon, Linda (2000), '"Irony, Nostalgia, and the Postmodern": Methods for the Study of Literature as Cultural Memory', *Studies in Comparative Literature* 30

Jacobs, Jason (2003), *Body Trauma TV: The New Hospital Dramas* (London: British Film Institute)

———— (2000), *The Intimate Screen: Early British Television Drama* (Oxford: Oxford University Press)

Johnson, Catherine (2005), *Telefantasy* (London: British Film Institute)

Johnson-Smith, Jan (2004), *American Science Fiction TV: Star Trek, Stargate and Beyond* (London: I.B.Tauris)

Liebes, Tamar, and Elihu Katz (1993), *The Export of Meaning: The Cross-Cultural Meanings of Dallas* (Cambridge: Polity Press/Blackwell)

Livingstone, Sonia, and Moira Bovill (eds.) (2001), *Children and their Changing Media Environment: A European Comparative Study* (New Jersey: Lawrence Erlbaum Associates)

Livingstone, Sonia, and Peter Lunt (1994), *Talk on Television: Audience Participation and Public Debate* (London: Routledge)

Lury, Karen (2005), *Interpreting Television* (London: Hodder Arnold)

Kilborn, Richard (2003), *Staging the Real: Factual TV Programming in the Age of Big Brother* (Manchester: Manchester University Press)

Marriott, Stephanie (2001), 'In Pursuit of the Ineffable: How Television Found the Eclipse but Lost the Plot', *Media Culture and Society*, vol. 23, no. 6, pp. 725–42

Marvin, Carolyn (1988), *When Old Technologies Were New: Thinking about Communications in the Late Nineteenth Century* (Oxford: Oxford University Press)

McCarthy, Anna (2001), *Ambient Television* (North Carolina: Duke University Press)

McLuhan, Marshall (1964), *Understanding Media* (London: Routledge)

Mellencamp, Patricia (ed.) (1990), *Logics of Television: Essays in Cultural Criticism* (Indiana University Press)

Messenger Davies, Maire (1989), *Television is Good for Kids* (London: Hilary Shipman)

Meyrowitz, Joshua (1985), *No Sense of Place: The Impact of Electronic Media on Social Behaviour* (Oxford: Oxford University Press)

Mittell, Jason (2004), *Genre and Television* (London: British Film Institute)

Moores, Shaun (2000), *Media and Everyday Life in Modern Society* (Edinburgh: Edinburgh University Press)

Moran, Albert, and Justin Malbon (2005), *Understanding the Global TV*

Format (Bristol: Intellect Books)

Neale, Steve (1999), *Genre and Hollywood* (London: Routledge)

Nelson, Robin (1997), *Television Drama in Transition: Forms, Values and Cultural Change* (Basingstoke: Macmillan)

Newcomb, Horace (2005), *Encyclopedia of Television* (New York: Fitzroy Dearborn/Museum of Broadcasting)

Peters, John Durham (2001) 'Witnessing', *Media, Culture and Society*, vol. 23 no. 6, pp.707–24.

——— (1999), *Speaking into the Air: A History of the Idea of Communication* (Chicago: Chicago University Press)

Roscoe, Jane and Craig Hight (2001), *Faking It: Mock-documentary and the Subversion of Factuality* (Manchester: Manchester University Press)

Rowe, Kathleen (1995), *The Unruly Woman: Gender and the Genres of Laughter* (Austin: University of Texas Press)

Scannell, Paddy (2007), *Communication in Theory* (London: Sage)

——— (1996), *Radio, Television and Modern Life* (Oxford: Blackwell)

——— (2004), 'What Reality Has Misfortune?', *Media, Culture and Society*, vol. 26, no. 4, pp. 573–84

——— (2000), 'For-anyone-as-someone structures', *Media, Culture and Society*, vol. 22, no. 1, pp. 5–24

Silverstone, Roger (2007), *Media and Morality: On the Rise of the Mediapolis* (Cambridge: Polity)

——— (1999), *Why Study the Media* (London: Sage)

——— (1994), *Television and Everyday Life* (London: Routledge)

Spigel, Lynn (1992), *Make Room for TV: Television and the Family Ideal in Post-War America* (Chicago: University of Chicago Press)

Spigel, Lynn, and Jan Olsen (2004), *Television after TV: Essays on a Medium in Transition* (Duke University Press)

Thompson, John B. (1995), *The Media and Modernity: A Social Theory of the Media* (Cambridge: Polity Press)

Thompson, Kristin (2003), *Storytelling in Film and Television* (Massachusetts: Harvard University Press)

Tomlinson, John (1991), *Cultural Imperialism: A Critical Introduction* (Johns Hopkins University Press)

Turnock, Rob (2007), *Television and Consumer Culture: Britain and the Transformation of Modernity* (London: I.B.Tauris)

Whannel, Garry (1992), *Fields in Vision: Television Sport and Cultural Transformation* (London: Routledge)

Williams, Raymond (2003), *Television: Technology and Cultural Form* (London: Routledge Classics)

Winston, Brian (2000), *Lies, Damn Lies and Documentaries* (London: British Film Institute)

——— (1998), *Media Technology and Society: A History from the Telegraph to the Internet* (London: Routledge)

Vinen, Richard (2002), *A History in Fragments: Europe in the Twentieth Century* (London: Abacus)

Where can I find out more?

Index